OSINT for the Staffing World

By Dean "The Search Authority" Da Costa with Derek "DZ" Zeller - Editor

Introduction

Hello, and welcome to the world of Dean Da Costa. You may know me by now as the tools guy. I have built, over the years, a reputation for knowing about all of the sourcing and recruiting tools out there and have been on multiple advisory boards helping guide companies and startups in the most efficient way to source and recruit candidates. I also wrote alot of words about other subjects in the world of recruiting and this to me is just that, a compilation of thoughts I think sharing would be fun to do and a good read for you to look at and use in the future. I hope you enjoy and learn from the world I have called my home, sourcing and recruiting.

I have been thinking long and hard about writing this and other books. Thanks to the love and support of my wife Bettina and the belief of my children Jeremy and Deanna, My granddaughter Heather, as well as the support of many of my friends. I want to take this time to recognize some of the people who have been instrumental in the writing of this and the other books and in my growth as a professional. First to the

ones who I learn from every day- Aaron
Lintz, Steve Levy, Marvin Smith, Derek
Zeller, Shannon Pritchard, Amybeth Quinn,
Pete Radloff, Susanna Frazier, Glenn
Gutmacher, Jeremy Roberts, Greg Hawkes,
Brett Fieg and so many more. Thanks to
all!!

Lastly, I asked Derek to help me edit this
and put it together for me as we have been
friends for years now and well, he is one hell
of a writer so why not lean on those who can
help you the most. So, thanks "DZ" you are
the best. Also, my daughter who is a writer
went over it. In addition, Michael
"BATMAN" Cohen who will now be known
as "The Editor-in-Cowl" also assisted in
editing the book.

Table of Contents

Chapter 1

Preface

This is a preface to the book, so you can understand what to expect and what I am trying to share. Over the years since my first presentation involving OSINT, much has been said, discussed, and thrown around about it. In some cases, with little regard for the understanding of the good, the bad, and the ugly, of OSINT. Also, with little consideration to understanding precisely what OSINT and other Intelligence categories are and can do.

This book is meant for the staffing industry. We will go over what most of the different kinds of intelligence are, what they do and even talk about a few tools in each. Once all of that is over, we will go more in-depth on OSINT, the types of OSINT, and some tools that you can use, how to use them, etc. In talking about tools, I will put them into categories of the type of OSINT they cover and if need be where they fit within the parts of the web ranging from "Level S"(LS) (ClearNet, this is where you spend most of your time) to "Level 5"(L5) (the Marianas Web, where you should never go).

This book is meant as a beginner's guide, that is in plain speak and hopefully will give you insights into the who, what, where, when and why of OSINT as well as some tools you can use. In some cases, the "chapters" are short, maybe even one page. I am not interested in overwhelming you with things that are not really important. All that said, some chapters will be huge, specifically the OSINT chapter, which is where we will spend most of our time.

The thing to remember about all the Intelligence categories to include OSINT is they all can and do overlap and intersect with each other, some more than others, such as OSINT and SOCMINT. Hopefully, when you are done with this book, you will have a decent plain speak understanding of all of this.

Chapter 2

Definitions You Need to Know

This is a list of definitions of words you will see in this book or words I think you should know. These are simple definitions, not meant to be dictionary style but in plain speak.

API (Application Programming Interface) - this is software that allows two applications to communicate with each other. They can be used to gather information.

ASINT- All Sources Intelligence.

CYBINT/DNINT - Cyber Intelligence/Digital Network Intelligence.

FININT (Financial Intelligence) - gathered from analysis of monetary transactions, statements etc.

GEOINT (Geospatial intelligence) - gathered from satellite, aerial photography, and mapping/terrain data combined with human activity analysis.

HUMINT (Human intelligence) - gathered from a person in the location in questioning and statements.

MASINT (Measurement and signature intelligence) - this includes but is not limited to RF, Nuclear, and more.

SIGINT - Signals intelligence - gathered from interception of signals this includes Communications, Electronic and more.

ELINT - Electronic Intelligence - part of SIGINT.

COMIT (Communications Intelligence) - part of SIGINT.

TECHINT (Technical intelligence) - gathered from analysis of weapons and equipment used by the armed forces of foreign nations, or environmental conditions as well as Medical called MEDINT which also falls under this category.

MEDINT (Medical Intelligence) - part of TECHINT.

S&TI (Scientific & Technical Intelligence) - part of TECHINT.

EI (Economic Intelligence) - part of TECHINT.

SOCMINT - is the analytical exploitation of information on Social Media.

IMINT - Image intelligence that combined with human activity analysis makes up GEOINT.

NCMI - National Center for Medical Intelligence.

DIA - Defense Intelligence Agency.

OSINT - Open Source Intelligence— gathered from open sources such as Facebook, LinkedIn, news groups, user groups, conferences, TV, reports, literature and more.

TOR Browser (onion routing) - is a browser designed for anonymous and secure web browsing. It was created by the US Navy, though it was designed to be more secure than virtually any other browser it is not immune to attack so additional security is recommended.

VPN (Virtual Private Network) - extends a private network across multiple networks. This also can mean your IP address changes. This gives you access to sites you may not have had access before all while hiding your real IP address and making it harder for people to find you.

IP Address - IP stand for Intern Protocol, and is a unique string of numbers that identifies your computer.

Virtual Machine - is software that like a physical computer runs an operating systems and corresponding applications.

International Organization of Standard (ISO) - an international standard organization.

ISO image - an ISO standard image of an operating system or software.

Staffing - for the purposes of this book this includes Sourcing, research, recruiting, interviewing and other like tasks, functions, and jobs.

UAV - Unmanned Aerial Vehicle.

GPS - Global Positioning System.

NGO - Non-Governmental Organizations.

POW - Prisoner of War.

JSTARS - Joint Surveillance Target Attack Radar System.

Malware - is software designed to disrupt, damage, destroy or gain unauthorized access to a system.

Virus - this is as it relates to a computer type system and it is designed to spread from host to host, replicating itself along the way. Think of it as a type of malicious code that will act on its own, attach itself to legitimate files and either start destroying things, copying things, or worse. There are many types of Viruses some of the most common are; Resident Virus, Multipartite Virus, Web Scripting, Browser Hijacker, Direct Action and many many more.

Phishing - is a fake way to obtain information such as user names, passwords and more by pretending to be a legitimate entity while involved in electronic communications.

Spyware - this is software that enables a person to obtain information from a system or systems, in a covert manner. This software is usually installed without the knowledge of the owner.

Botnets - this may be the least heard of threat. It is a collection of software that created an army of infected computers known as "Zombies'. This army is also called a "Hive". They can send spam emails with viruses attached, spread Malware and more.

Distributed denial-of-service (DDoS) attack - this is when the owner of a "Zombie" gets his whole "Hive" to attack a specific website or server. Think about it as an all-out attack. What it can do it close down a site or system, making it hard to get your request through.

Hacking - this is gaining unauthorized access to a site, or system. It is also when you get information from a site or system in a way in which it was not meant to be gotten. A low low-level example is x-raying.

Pharming - this is the creation of fake, malicious, or illegitimate websites and redirecting people to these sites, whereby they require or request personnel information. These threats spook the real site as close as possible.

Ransomware - this is a type of malware that restricts access to your files and programs unless you make some kind of payment.

Spam - this is perhaps the most common threat, basically it is receiving unauthorized or ask for electronic communication.

Spoofing - this threat is often used in conjunction with Phishing. It is when they create a website or email address that is very similar to the real one, and makes it look like it came from a legitimate source.

Trojan Horse - this is a malicious program that is embedded within legitimate software. It has an executable file that will install itself and run automatically. It can delete your files, use your computer to gain access to others computers, watch you through a webcam, and much more. This threat is one of the worse.

Wi-Fi Eavesdropping - the threat here is someone listening in on information you are sharing over an unsecure Wi-Fi.

Worms - these are alot like viruses, except that it will go to work on its own, without needing to be attached to file or program.

WPA2 Handshake Vulnerabilities - this is what's called a "Key Reinstallation attack (Krack). Krack vulnerabilities allow a bad guy or malicious attacker to read the encrypted network traffic on a WIFI protected access (WPA2) router.

NSA (National Security Agency) - this is the national intelligence agency in the US.

CIA (Central Intelligence Agency) - this is the foreign intelligence service of the US government.

FBI (Federal Bureau of Investigation) - this is the domestic intelligence and security arm of the US.

OSS (Office of Strategic Services) - this was the first wartime intelligence agency in the US.

Penetration Tester (Pen Tester) - this is someone who will conduct authorized simulated cyberattack on a computer for the purposes of evaluating the security of systems.

Hacker - is a person who uses a computer to gain information in a way in which it was not designed to be gotten or in an unauthorized way.

White Hat Hacker - this is an internet slang term for an Ethical Hacker. Ethical Hackers specialize in pen testing. Otherwise call the good guys.

Black Hat Hacker - this is the bad guy who tries to illegally violate the computer security of a person or entity for malicious purposes.

Grey Hat Hacker - like in life things are seldom black and white. So too is the world of Hacking. A Gray Hat hacker is someone who lives in both worlds. Think of them as blackmailers of sorts. What they might do is look for vulnerabilities in a system. If they find one, they might let the owner know and request a small fee. If they don't get the fee, they will post the vulnerability on the web for all to see. Now this is the exception to the rule as most Grey Hats do not share the information they find, however since they are doing the hacking without permission it is not legal, but since they are not doing anything with what they find it is also not truly bad, hence that fine line.

BBC - this is the British Broadcasting Corporation, which is a British public service broadcaster.

Metadata - this is data about data. It is the data that is contained in web pages, documents, pictures, files and nearly anything you find on the net.

Burner Computer - this is a term for a computer that you use in place of your normal computer.

Linux - this is a free open source software operating system that is heavily command line focused. Most OSINT tools are Linux based.

Penetration Testing – this is also called Pen Testing or Ethical Hacking (see below).

Ethical Hacking - the good guys. Sometimes called Penetration Testing or Pen Testing (see above) their main job is to find information, vulnerabilities, and threats and might recommend counter measures. What the White hat hackers do.

Research - this is the investigation of materials, and sources to establish facts to reach conclusions or lead to further avenues of research.

Investigation - this is the act of using a formal or systematic approach to find the, who, what, when, how or why of the subject.

DNS (Domain Name System) - this is a hierarchical and decentralized naming system for computers, services, and other resources connected to the internet.

Whois - this is a type of lookup that can tell you information about an IP address such as owner, maybe email and phone and more.

Port Scanners - these are tools that can tell you what services are associated with what services and also reveal a possible vulnerability.

Google Search syntax - this includes Boolean, google dorks, and more.

Python - this is an easy to learn programming language that is used with alot of OSINT tools.

Cache - this is a hardware or software component that stores data based on requests. This data can and often includes older data, even data that may have been removed by the host system.

Proxy Server - this is a server that acts as an intermediary between the user computer and the internet. It adds an extra layer and some security.

Lifecycle/Methodology - you will see these two terms interchanged. For the purposes of this book they are one and the same.

Keep in mind there will be other definitions throughout this book, but these are some you may need to know up front. That said most can be looked up rather easily. Also, here are some other reference materials you may want to get as well based on the definitions and some really good source material.

"The Book of Recruiting; Da Costa Style"- my book on Recruiting which you can find on Amazon.

Tool - for the purposes of this book a tool is a system, site, method, program or app that helps us accomplish a task.

What Everybody is Saying by Joe Navarro - a great book about nonverbal communication for use in HUMINT and Staffing.

Chapter 3

Levels of the Web

So, the Web/Internet has multiple levels to it. Though most only go to the very top part. There are varying opinions about how many levels there are and what each level means, the ones I mention below appear to be the most prevailing opinion by most of the top experts. These levels are equated to the levels of the ocean starting with what we see above the water and going to the very depths of the deepest part of the ocean.

Level 0 (L0) or Common Web or Clearnet - is the part above the water. This includes; Social Networks, most Search Engines, Wiki Encyclopedia, Email Services, common internet services and the like.

Level 1 (L1) or Surface Web - is that part just below the surface and include; Blogs, Essays, Temp Email Services, Closed Social Networks, Simple AI, Hosting Services, Reddit, Forums, University Databases, Alexa Ranking, Tumblr, Amazon/Ebay, and more.

90+% of the web lies below this point!

Level 2 (L2) or Bergie Web - is that part of the web that sits below L1 but before the level you should use a Proxy to get into. This level includes; Ad popups, Google Locked results, Web Archives, Anon Boards, Torrents B2B, Wikileaks, and alot more.

Proxy Service recommended starting here.

Level 3 (L3) or Deep Web - is the part where you are starting to get into the serious part of the web. The part where you could see things you do not want to see. This includes; Spambots, Spiders, Scandals, Virtual Reality, Hacking Guides, Script Kiddies, and more.

TOR Services Required starting Here

Level 4 (L4) or Charter Web or Dark Web - is the part of the web where you start seeing things that border on or are illegal. This includes; banned media, rare animal trade, corporate exchanges, most ". onion" addresses and more.

Level 5 (L5) or Marianas Web - this is the part of the web that in some ways is a myth, but not the good kind.

Now keep in mind, while I pointed out you need a TOR browser after L3, and proxy after L2 that does not mean you cannot or should not use a proxy starting at L1. As you will see in the chapter on VPN, there are some huge advantages to using a VPN.

There are some thoughts that there are 2 more levels. The prevailing experts say these levels are part of the Marianas Web. That said just as an FYI here they are:

Level 6&7 - The Fog/Virus Soup this is more of a stop over as you try to get to Level 8

Level 8 - The Primarch System this is what controls the internet itself. This is the most heavily secured area on the net. It has what is called level 17 quantum function lock, and is virtually impossible to break even by the best hackers.

Chapter 4

TOR

TOR stands for "The Onion Router". This is the browser you need to access online services without revealing your identity. It was initially released in 2002, as part of the TOR project. Its most recent release was Dec 2018 and currently can be run on Microsoft, Mac, Android, Linux and most Unix-like systems. Basically, it is what you need to access the deep and dark web. Onion sites are those sites that are primarily in the Deep and Dark parts of the web.

So, the Deep Web, which includes the Dark Web, is estimated to be over 500X bigger than what we normally see. It makes up 96% of the web. Some of the things it can do are:

Block trackers and ads from following you where you go on the net.

Defend against surveillance - it stops people from following your search patterns, all anyone can see is your using TOR.

Resist Fingerprinting - TOR makes all users look the same therefore making it hard for someone to find your digital fingerprint

Encryption - TOR takes encryption to a new level by encrypting what you do 3 times as it passes over the network.

IP Randomizing - this means changing your IP address at specific intervals. TOR comes set to change every 10 minutes but you can change that to virtually anything you want.

Browsing Freely - TOR allows you to browse freely and see sites that may have been blocked to your home network. It so secure that even the National Security Agency (NSA) has struggled to identify TOR users.

Tor2web - is a site where you can find some onion sites; but not the same as using a TOR browser. However, if you add ".to" to the end of the URL you are looking at you can see the actual TOR page.

Is TOR legal? Yes, you use it like any other browser.

Who uses TOR and these other options? Military, Police, journalist, and some more famous or infamous people like Julian Assange. Unfortunately, like anything that is good, there are some that proliferate it, so you have the drug dealers, arms dealers, and much more dark types using it as well. The creation and maturation of Bitcoin has only made it worse as people can now buy things with crypto- currency that is virtually untraceable.

The TOR Browser can be found at: ** https://www.torproject.org/download/

So, when you decide to get TOR you will have some choices to make. You can download it for; Windows, Apple, Android, and Linux. It can be downloaded in multiple languages to include: English, German, Spanish, Italian, Portuguese, and others.

Installing it on Windows is very simple, and the directions are on the TOR site. However, let's go through it; simply download it to your computer. Then click on it and let the installer do its thing. Once it is installed and you open it, the first thing you will see is the connection wizard. Now you will have 2 choices, the first is when your internet connection is clear of obstacles, meaning things like company security. The 2nd is if you do have some issues and it will allow you to configure it manually.

When you are downloading it, you will notice other...variations and tools. These include:

Nyx - a command line monitor for TOR.

Orbot - a TOR for Android, sort of it is a free proxy app that allows apps to use the internet more securely (see next chapter on VPN).

Tails - a live operating systems that can be run from a USB. Its main thing is the added privacy that it allows.

TorBirdy - is an extension for Mozilla that enhances privacy.

Onionoo – this is a web-based tool, that can let you know who is currently running TOR relays, and bridges.

TOR Metrics - is a simple a way to see the usage metrics of TOR.

Pluggable Transports - is a tool that can help you get around censors who may be monitoring internet traffic.

Shadow - is a tool that lets you run real applications in a simulated internet environment.

Now truth be told none of the above tools are things a Staffing Professional will need, But I wanted you to know about them. There are other options for TOR, but they are far less used. Some of these are discussed below:

I2P - the invisible internet project is an anonymous network that allows anonymous messaging to other people. It can also be used to house anonymous websites, and more. It can be downloaded for Windows, Apple, Android, Linux, and more. It can be found at the url: https://geti2p.net/en/download

Freenet - is a peer to peer platform for censorship resistant communication. It lets you share files, browse, chat, and publish free sites without censorship. Because Freenet is decentralized it is less vulnerable to attacks. It can also be used in the "darknet" mode where you are only connected to your friends. https://freenetproject.org/pages/download.html

There are tools that come with TOR built in. I will mention a few here, but will talk more in depth on them later in the OSINT chapter, and for some of the tools in their own chapter.

OSIRT - this stands for "Open Source Internet Research Tool", and is an all in one research tool, used by investigators for OSINT research. It comes with TOR built in and ready to go. There will be more on that later. More on this in Chapter 26. **

Red Onion - is a TOR powered web browser. This browser is built for anonymous browsing and the darknet. It is an IOS program and works on most IOS systems

The Onion Browser Button - this is a Chrome Extension that allows you to browse the web using a TOR proxy.

Buscador - this is what I call "The Answer". Simply put this is the premier, OSINT tool out there as it comes with everything to include TOR. There will be more on this in chapter 28.**

I definitely believe you should have TOR, as it will help you with your research and with staying private.

Chapter 5

Virtual Private Network (VPN)

A VPN is a secure tunnel between two or more devices from various locations that create a secure environment to protect privacy and interference. One of the main ways a VPN helps is that it will show your IP address as someplace else from where you are. So that means if someone is trying to see where you are located, they will likely see you in a different location since you are using a VPN. In some cases, a VPN can have a rotational capability which means it will change IP address and locations at different intervals. Some of the things a VPN can do for you is;

- allow you to see things on the net that normally you can't due to location.
- avoid slowdowns.
- avoid 3rd party apps and stuff from spying,.
- safely connect to any WIFI.
- hide who you are when researching other companies or people.
-

Now since you just read about TOR the next question is why do you need a VPN if you use TOR. Well the correct question is can you use both? The answer is YES. Think about it a secure, IP Address changing VPN, while using TOR. That is a whole lot of ability to search while being close to as safe as you can be.

So below are a few of the better VPNs that you can use. Some are free, some are fermium, and some are cost. Alot are Chrome extensions.

ProtonVPN - one of the best and most secured VPNs out there. There are 4 different plans that range from free-24 a month. **

ExpressVPN - free for 30 days, unlimited, has Chrome, Safari, and Firefox extensions, has servers in 27 US and over 90 countries.

CyberGhost - free for 45 days, 60+ countries, and malware protection.

Surfshark - 50+ countries, 30 days free, unlimited & private P2P/Torrenting.

Hotspot Shield - 25+ countries, free for 45 days.

Free VPN - a chrome ext, totally free, 90+ countries, and more. **

Brosec - a chrome ext, has both free and paid, more than 90 countries

uVPN - a free VPN with unlimited usage, over 90+ countries, the ability to rotate or choose, and much more.

Here is a pretty extensive list of other VPNs:

- 12VPN
- Adtelly
- AirVPN
- Anonymous VPN
- Avast SecureLine VPN
- Avira Phantom VPN
- Banana VPN
- BartVPN
- BolehVPN
- boxpn
- BTGuard
- Buffered VPN
- CactusVPN

- EarthVPN
- Easy Hide IP
- Encrypt.me
- F-Secure Freedome
- FastestVPN
- FrootVPN
- GhostPath
- GOOSE VPN
- GoTrusted
- HashtagVPN
- Hide My IP
- Hide.me
- HideIPVPN
- HideMyAss
- ibVPN
- Internetz.me
- IPVanish
- IronSocket
- Ivacy
- iVPN
- Kepard
- Le VPN
- Leafy VPN
- Liberty Shield
- LiquidVPN
- MyVPN
- NoodleVPN
- NordVPN
- OneVPN Money Back Guarantee
- OverPlay
- OVPN

- Panda VPN
- Perfect Privacy
- Perimeter 81 Free Trial
- Perimeter 81
- PrimeVPN
- Private Internet Access
- Private WiFi
- proXPN
- Proxy.sh
- ProxyServer.com
- PureVPN
- SaferVPN
- SecureTunnel
- Shellfire VPN
- SlickVPN
- Speedify Review
- SpyOff
- StrongVPN
- SurfEasy
- SwissVPN
- SwitchVPN
- tigerVPN
- TorGuard
- TorVPN
- Total VPN
- Trust.Zone
- TunnelBear
- USAIP.eu
- VersaVPN
- VPN Traffic
- VPN Unlimited

- VPN.ac
- VPN.asia
- VPN.ht
- VPN4ALL
- VPNArea
- VPNGhost
- VPNhub
- VPNLand
- VPNSecure
- VyprVPN
- Windscribe
- WorldVPN
- ZenMate
- ZenVPN
- ZPN

Chapter 6

Virtual Machines (VMs)

A Virtual Machine (VM) is software that like a physical computer runs an operating systems and corresponding applications. This allows you to run multiple operating systems on one computer, while isolating each one from not just the host but each other as well. VMs can be divided into 2 categories' System Virtual Machines (SVM) and Process Virtual Machines (PVM).

SVMs - is a platform that supports sharing of physical computers resources between what could be multiple VMs. This is done by a virtualization technique provided by a software layer known as Hypervisor.

PVMs - are designed to provide platform independence.

Reasons for using a VM vary. Some of the best are:

1. Allows for multiple operating systems on the same machine, while also keeping them separate.

2. VMs are easily available and easy to maintain.
3. VMs also act as a bit of a sandbox, isolating these systems from the host and protecting the host.
4. VMs also provide disaster recovery options.

Some drawbacks include:

1. They are not as efficient and as such they might be slower
2. Running too many at one time can cause some instability.

Now of course these VMs can run on desktop, and Servers.

Some of the better Virtual Machine software is:

VMware Player - is a FREEWARE for personal use software that will allow you to mount and run VMs directly from a Windows or Linux desktop.

Parallels - is full-featured virtual machine software.

Microsoft Hyper-V - once upon a time there was Microsoft VirtualPC, then there was Microsoft VirtualServer, and now there's Microsoft Hyper-V.

VirtualBox - FREE virtual machine software if you're looking for an alternative to VMware Workstation. And it's an excellent choice for beginners. ** This is my preferred Virtual Machine; the instructions for installation is simple and easy and found on the site where you download the program.

Of course, there are others, but these are the best and easiest.

Once you have VM software you can create VMs that can run; Linux, UNIX, Windows, Mac, Android and virtually any operating system out there. ISOs for all these operating systems can be found on the web for the specific VM you are using, as well as instructions on how to do it.

These VMs are particularly useful and in my mind required when in the deep and dark web.

Chapter 7

Sandbox

Sandbox often called Sandboxing is a strategy that isolates applications, testing, and other activities from critical systems and the base operating system (OS). Some of the reasons for Sandboxing is:

Security - because a sandbox environment does not have free access to the base OS, apps and such, it addresses a level of security.

Testing - using sandboxing for testing allows you to test in anyway, without concern for the base OS.

Plan Updates/Training - sandboxing would allow you to let people play with an upcoming update or new system without concerns for it impacting the base OS or system.

Now as you can imagine if you were to really want to be safe and secure you could run TOR in a Virtual Machine, using a VPN all sitting in a sandboxed environment.

Some Sandbox tools are;

BitBox (Browser in a Box) - this is specifically designed for web browsing in a sandbox environment.

BufferZone - this is an endpoint sandbox tool. If you plan on heading into the dangerous parts of the web, L2 and below, you should consider using this tool.

SandBoxie - this is one of the most popular and most used sandbox tools. It isolates everything from the base OS. **

SHADE Sandbox - this is a very very simple and easy to use free sandboxing tool. **

Toolwiz Time Freeze - this tool works much differently and in truth is barley a sandbox tool. It actually makes a complete copy of your entire OS, files and saves that state. After doing whatever it is you wanted to do in a sandbox environment, simply restart your computer and your original system will be restored with no sign of the work you did.

Shadow Defender - this tool is just like Toolwiz Time Freeze.

Chapter 8

Burner Computer - Linux

A burner computer is a computer you use in place of your primary one. Similar to a burner phone this is done so it cannot be easily traced. People who perform OSINT will use these computers so they can stay "off the grid", which means hard to find and trace. In most cases these machines will be Linux as most heavy-duty OSINT tools are Linux based.

Now of course as you read in the previous chapter you can use a Virtual Machine that can allow you to run Linux. However, some deep diving people prefer Linux and therefore use a burner computer.

Now there are alot of different "flavors" of Linux you can use, these include:

Ubuntu - this is by far the most popular version. Ubuntu include such popular tools as Firefox and OpenOffice. It has a 6-month release cycle that seems to be pretty consistent. There have been some ...spinoffs of it such as Kubuntum, Xubuntu and Lubuntu, but Ubuntu remains the standard.

Fedora - this is a free version of Red Hat called RHEL (Red Hat Enterprise Linux). It also has a 6-month release cycle, and has excellent security features.

Linux Mint – this s a version that adds it's own desktop, has some added graphic tools, and is set up for easier installation.

Debian - this is perhaps the most tested and bug free version of Linux. It has slow release cycles and can be harder to achieve compatibility.

Now of course there are specialized versions. These versions are of interest to us as it relates to OSINT. Some of them are:

Kali Linux - this is the ethical hacking and penetration OS. It comes loaded with alot of penetration testing tools, as well as other things. This is based on the Debian version of Linux. **

BackBox - is an Ubuntu based Linux system. It was developed for penetration testing and security assessment.

Parrot Security OS - This is a relatively new Linux OS. It is based on Debian and is designed for cloud-based penetration testing.

Samurai Web Testing Framework - is designed, well as it says Web Testing. Unlike the others this comes as a Virtual Machine (see previous chapter). It is based on Ubuntu.

There are many others to include some specific to OSINT we will discuss later.

Chapter 9

Intelligence VS Staffing

Intelligence is the information gathered from an intelligence investigation. What this entails depends on what kind of intelligence investigation; meaning as an example HUMINT or GEOINT. All that said there are certain processes that are consistent regardless of the type of intelligence investigation. The main process itself is consistent throughout any type of investigation. That process or lifecycle is:

Intelligence Gathering - this is where you gather the information

Analysis - you analyze the information to determine what to do next.

Action items or next steps - this is what happens next and can be more intelligence gathering but more targeted, it can be a final determination, it can be a defense strategy that someone else implements.

Now what is interesting is that, this process is actually the same as parts of the staffing lifecycle, Specifically as part of the sourcing lifecycle, which I outlined in my book "The book of Recruiting Da Costa Style". So, the sourcing lifecycle short version is:

Research - includes internal and external and analysis.

Source - finding resumes, bio, lists etc.

Download or Scrape - getting the info out of where ever it is.

Enhancement - find more info like email or phone.

Outreach - contacting the people.

Now there are other steps in the staffing lifecycle of which the sourcing life cycle is part of. The reason the sourcing lifecycle as I define it stops at outreach is because not all sourcers do more than this, some reach out in the name of a recruiter who screens them, and others screen them themselves.

So, let's look at the sourcing lifecycle and were the pats of the intelligence lifecycle fit:

Research - we are doing research both internally and externally to determine what we are looking for, salary, background etc. Out of this would come a sourcing plan to act upon. This is consistent with the Intelligence Gathering and Analysis part of the Intelligence lifecycle.

Sourcing + downloading/scraping + enhancement - this is where we actually find perspective candidates, gather the information we have and look to enhance it. This is consistent with the Intelligence Gathering, analysis and action items part of the Intelligence lifecycle.

Outreach - this is where we analyze all the data to come up with the best outreach method and we implement that method. This is consistent with the Intelligence Gathering and Analysis part if the Intelligence lifecycle.

Now the intelligence lifecycle can also be used in other parts of the staffing lifecycle, as the end game for those steps are the same as the end game for the staffing lifecycle steps.

Chapter 10

ASINT - All Sources Intelligence

ASINT is basically the uber name for all intelligence. All forms of intelligence falls under this umbrella. Under this are three distinct types of intelligence that all categories fall under. They are;

General Public - this is things easily found right in plain sight.

Nonpublic - this is things that are harder to find

Specialized Public - these are things that are highly specific and as such is the hardest to find.

Some of the categories of ASINT are:

Humint
IMINT
GEOINT
MASINT
SIGNIT
TECHINT
MEDINT
FIINIT
CYBINT

SOCMINT
OSINT

Keep in mind within these categories can be subcategories. Also the varying responsibilities and tools of these categories also stretch over to others. So, you might read similar things more than once. In addition, most of these categories are interdependent of each other. As an example, you can't have GEOINT without IMINT.

All Intelligence will have certain steps or a lifecycle. This lifecycle is very simple but very important and was outlined in the previous chapter.

For us and this book we will hit SOCMINT and OSINT first as these apply to the research, source, and enhancement part of the methodology/lifecycle and then HUMINT as it is mainly the engagement and interviewing part of the methodology/lifecycle which comes after the research, sourcing and enhancement parts.

All of this and more is explained further in this book.

Chapter 11

GEOINT (Geospatial intelligence)

Geospatial intelligence is intelligence about human activity on earth gathered from the analysis of satellite, aerial photography, mapping, and terrain data. This includes 3D rendering. It is the combination of IMINT and human activity analysis of a given geographical point or place.

This includes the exploitation and analysis of all this data. With the idea to describe, assess, and visually depict the features of buildings, mountains, and other physical features both natural and manmade. Where this comes in handy is when planning out an attack or defense.

Prior to being given the name GEOINT in 2003, GEOINT was simply part of the National Imagery and Mapping Agency (NIMA) and had no designation.

GEOINT has become so big since then you can actually get a certificate on it from many schools to include the University of Missouri. There is even an accrediting body called the United States Geospatial Intelligence Foundation (USGIF)

One type of GEOINT or rather the info that falls under GEOINT can also be provided by means such as UAV (Unmanned Aerial Vehicle). Now I understand you could say that is Aerial photography, however UAV is well UAV.

We all watch the TV, and see and hear about airstrikes, missile build up, and the like going on around. All of that intelligence is coming from satellite surveillance of which most is GEOINT based. Another thing to consider is the intelligence could also be using various tools that can provide depth of masses and density, such as using sonar probes. For those that are not aware and own drones, well if you have a camera on it and take video or pictures, guess what? GEOINT.

GEOINT is such a big part of the intelligence community it has its own symposiums, conferences, certification and the like. As to tools that can help you here, we are talking about things like:

GPS Visualizer

Creepy - We will get into this one later in chapter 24.**

Tools that track aircraft, ships, trains, etc.

Most mapping tools

Satellite tools such as Earth Explorer which can give you a satellite view of any point on earth, from virtually any given date and time. TerraServer like Earth Explorer it can provide up to date satellite images of virtually any place on earth. We will touch much more on this in the OSINT chapter.

Chapter 12

IMINT - Imagery Intelligence

IMINT is closely related to GEOINT in that you need IMINT to perform GEOINT. IMINT is one half the requirements of GEOINT. IMINT is the collecting of information from satellite and aerial photography.

Examples of ways in which we gather IMINT are;

UAVs (Unmanned Aerial Vehicles).

JSTARS (Joint Surveillance Target Attack Radar System).

Satellites - commercial and military.

Film, Digital, and Video; both civilian and military.

These types of images can be collected via; visual photography, Visual recording, infrared, lasers, multi-spectral sensors, sonar and radar. Now I know this seems very closely related to GEOINT as I said but GEOINT is more related to Security while IMINT is not. Also, GEOINT also includes the analysis of the intelligence that IMINT and

GEOINT gather. GEOINT focuses on human activity while IMINT is all nonhuman activity, for example monitoring of geological areas of concern such as a volcano.

Tools that we may have access to that fit this category are:

Google Earth - satellite view of earth and locations. **

Paliscope - a photo forensic tool. **

GEO Search tool for YouTube - search you tube videos vie location tags.

Persisearch - a periscope location search and many more. **

Chapter 13

MASINT (Measurement and Signature Intelligence)

MASINT is scientific and technical intelligence information obtained by both quantitative and qualitative analysis of data that falls into several categories such as; metric, angle, spatial, wavelength, time dependence, modulation, plasm, hydro magnetic and more. Each of the categories of course has their own sub category of intelligence;

- Radar Intelligence (RADINT)
- Acoustic Intelligence (ACOUSTINT)
- Nuclear Intelligence (NUCINT)
- Radio Frequency/Electromagnetic Pulse Intelligence (RF/EMPINT)
- Electro-optical Intelligence (ELECTRO-OPTINT)
- Laser Intelligence (LASINT)
- Materials Intelligence
- Unintentional Radiation Intelligence (RINT)
- Chemical and Biological Intelligence (CBINT)
- Directed Energy Weapons Intelligence (DEWINT)

- Effluent/Debris Collection
- Spectroscopic Intelligence
- Infrared Intelligence (IRINT)

In addition to the subcategories listed above you have 6 major disciplines that fall under MASINT and as you might guess there is some overlap. They are:

Materials MASINT - this is the collecting, processing and analyzing of pas, liquid and solid samples. This is critical in the defense of chemical, biological, and radiological threats (CBR).

Electro-optical MASINT - this is the intelligence gathering activities that bring together elements that do not fit into other related categories.

Nuclear MASINT - this covers measurement and characterization of information derived from nuclear radiation, and other physical phenomena associated with nuclear orientated things.

Geophysical MASINT - this involves phenomena transmitted through the earth (ground, water or atmosphere) and manmade structures.

Radar MASINT (RADINT) - this is the intelligence gathering activities that bring together elements that do not fit into other related categories.

Radiofrequency MASINT - this focuses on the unintentionally transmitted information unlike, COMINT and ELINT, which are sub parts of SIGINT and deal with intentionally transmitted things.

Electromagnetic Pulse (EMP) MASTINT - this focuses on the EMP that comes with the aftermath of the use of nuclear weapons, and other EMP causing events.

As you can see it is a very large set of intelligence. The idea is to identify distinctive characteristics of fixed or moving targets. So, as an example you could use MASINT intelligence to help aim munitions or find enemy troops or potential threats and such. I am not going to go into detail on each one as none are relevant to Staffing, Sourcing or Recruiting.

Most tools in this category are not software tools or things that the staffing world uses. That said a few are:

RF Spectrum Analyzer - this tool analyzes the RF signal.

Gieger Counter - this tool measures nuclear based energy

Chapter 14

SIGINT (Signals Intelligence)

SIGINT is intelligence gathered by the interception of signals. This includes signals between machines, and people. If it is machines it is called ELINT or Electronic Intelligence. If it is people, it is called COMIT or Communications Intelligence. Since alot of the information gathered this way is sensitive and often encrypted is also involves the use of Cryptanalysis.

A thing to remember is that in some cases the traffic of communication, it's the who, what, where, when, and why that can yield alot of information. Also keep in mind communications can take on many forms, such as: written, verbal, non-verbal to include sign language, Morse Code both visual and auditory, and more.

A place where this hits for staffing is in the communications side. As staffing professionals, we rely on our ability to communicate and read between the lines when talking with candidates and hiring managers alike. It also relates to Staffing this type of SIGNIT is also covered in the HUMINT chapter as this is where SIGNIT and HUMINT overlap. In my first book "Recruiting Da Costa Style" I spoke about Lookology and Lisology, which are techniques you use when speaking with candidates and hiring managers in person or on the phone to help you garner needed information to either find candidates or decipher if a candidate you are talking to is a fit. For us as staffing professionals this is the part of the staffing lifecycle that fits at the beginning when you are doing an intake, at the middle when you are doing your initial screens, and at the end when final interviews happen. In the end all of these things are about gathering intelligence. As for tools that you can use for staffing it would include video interviewing such as:

Hirevue

Sparkhire

VidCruiter

Note taking tools such as:

    Word **

    Edit pad **

Conferencing tools some of which provide notes such as:

    Zoom **

    Uber **

    Join.me

Chapter 15

TECHINT (Technical Intelligence)

This category of intelligence is mainly focused on intelligence about weapons, and equipment used by the armed forces. Within this lies three sub categories which are: S&TI (Scientific and Technical Intelligence), MEDINT (Medical Intelligence) and EI (Economic Intelligence).

S&TI (Scientific and Technical Intelligence) - this is intelligence gathered from the collection, evaluation and interpretation of foreign scientific and technical information.

EI (Economic Intelligence) - this is the intelligence gathered from covertly obtaining data, policy, and proprietary information that can impact a country's economic standing.

MEDINT (Medical Intelligence) - this is the intelligence gathered from the collection of, analysis of, foreign medical, bio-scientific, and environmental information. There will be more on this in the next chapter.

Keep in mind TECHINT and its sub categories can include both current information and historical. The reason for historical is past behaviors can be an indication of future actions. For the purposes of staffing this has no real impact as we are not trying to gain intelligence on a foreign country or power.

Some tools or collection techniques that are used with this are:

Spyware - allowing for spying on some person or entity.

Malware - this is designed to cause damage but can also be used to gather information.

Hacking - well simple enough getting into a system in a way it was not designed to get into and taking information.

Conventions - attending conventions and talking and listening this actually is also a place where HUMINT comes in handy.

Now, some companies have taken TECHINT to a whole new level. While TECHINT is technically for armed forces, specifically of other countries, some companies have applied these principles to what they are calling Competitive Technical Intelligence (CTI). Basically, this is their process of seeking to identify a competitor's technical R&D strategy and innovation pipeline to identify the next generation of threats in the marketplace. An example identifying the threats that might exist in the vulnerabilities of a competitor's product like the new apple phone if you are working for a company making google phones. This could give you incites as to how somebody or bodies might attack a competitor and this would lead you to ensure that same vulnerability does not exist in your product. CTI is not any kind of national security intelligence or espionage, nor is it any kind of industrial espionage. This intelligence is done using ethical and legal means. An example is attending a conference where they show the new product.

The researchers who conduct CTI created a three-level model comprising the framework, system, and process of acquiring technology intelligence. The government has even gone so far as to invest in the creation of Technology Forecasting Tools. These tools help to forecast technology's future characteristics or applications. Of course, even though it started with the government, civilian companies have also started doing this, using the intelligence gathered with CTI to help predict the technology of the future.

Chapter 16

MEDINT (Medical Intelligence)

MEDINT, as discussed in the last chapter on TECHINT, is the gathering of intelligence from the collection and analysis of foreign medical, bio-scientific, and environmental information.

Now MEDINT was not the only subcategory under TECHINT. However, I believe it may be the most important and as such is getting its own chapter. The reason for me it is the most essential subcategory is, this is where the intelligence on possible chemical and biological weapons would be found.

As someone who has fought in a war where weapons such as these where used, I can tell you the intelligence we got helped us not have more significant issues than we had. There is an actual organization whose charter is MEDINT it is called the National Center for Medical Intelligence (NCMI). This agency is a component of the Defense Intelligence Agency (DIA).

Another reason for this to have its own chapter is that this agency also monitors health threats for our country. This includes any outbreaks of past, present, or new health concerns. These include health concerns spread through direct or indirect contact, via droplet (via short distance mucosal surfaces, i.e., bathroom or when someone coughs), via a vector (via insects like a flea, tick, or mosquito) and via the airborne route. For those of you who are Zombie Apocalypse people, this is the agency that would first deal with this possibility.

What's interesting about MEDINT is we are surrounded by it. The watches, pendants and devices we use to monitor our steps, heart rate, pulse, etc. are all MEDINT. The sites we go on to see our medical records are MEDINT. There is even a company named MEDINT, who you guessed it they are in the medical data business, ensuring both patients and doctors can get quick access to the required records. There are not many tools specific to MEDINT, mostly it is any medical tool, and primary investigative methodologies and processes.

Chapter 17

FININT (Financial Intelligence)

FININT is the finding, and gathering of information related to financial matters of a given person or organization. An example of this might be identifying government employees who might owe alot of money and be easily influenced to do things if offered money, or government employees who may have made alot of money from foreign means and there for be corruptible by them. Besides knowing who might owe what, and where they are getting their money from, you can also see where the money is going, and see patterns that might tell us what a person's habits are, like where they eat, where they drink, etc.

You might also be able to see their stock trading habits and incites about them having any insider info. Also, in the case of foreign governments, you might see where they are getting their money. In the case of radicals, terrorists, and the like you might see who is funding them. For us, in staffing, of course, it can really help us, for example finding out current salary ranges. Seeing what companies are getting funding, and maybe even how they are spending it. We can also see how much money they are making; this can go a long way in predicting possible layoffs and such. Also finding out the total compensation they are offering.

Tools that are used with FININT vary, and I will talk mainly about the ones we might use in staffing, but there are many others.

Paysa - gives salary ranges. **

Salary.com - give salary ranges. **

Comparably - compares salaries by job, location, company, etc. **

Levels - comparing levels at different companies and salary ranges. **

Payscale - salary ranges, cost of living, charts, comparison between cities, and much more. **

Your Worth - tells you what you are worth, has a Chrome Ext.

CBInsights - tells you every company worth over 1billion and how much they are worth.

Craft - lets you compare companies' growth to include financial.

DataUSA - salary info, company info, etc.

Bureau of Labor and Statistics -lots of great info.

Crunchbase - can show recent funding.

AngelList - you can get all kinds of info on, acquisitions, financing and more with all the numbers involved.

Glassdoor - lots of stuff to include salary.

SalaryList - salary info and more.

Salary Expert - as it says.

HomeFair - the cost of living calculator.

Smart Asset - the cost of living calculator.

BankRate - calculators for the cost of living and much more.

NerdWallet - the cost of living calculator and the ability to compare between cities.

Recap.Work - a chrome ext that will show you salary range son Linkedin.

Chapter 18

CYBINT (Cyber Intelligence)

CBINT is the gathering of overt and covert information and materials, as well as the analyzing and evaluation of that information to produce intelligence products that would be critical to the assessment of vulnerabilities, threats and helping to assure the survivability of military and high-end systems. Traditional Intelligence gathering disciplines cannot address or keep up with the fast growth and constant ascension of cyberspace technologies.

Unlike most Intelligence CYBINT is a product, not an isolated Intelligence. In most cases, we are talking Survivability and Vulnerability, this includes:

Detectability - how well can the system avoid being identified.

Susceptibility - the ability of the system to avoid an attack.

Vulnerability - the ability of the system to withstand an attack.

Recoverability - the ability of the system to recover from an attack and return to the fully functional and capable state.

So basically, we are talking avoiding, withstanding, and recovering from an attack.

As I am sure by now, you can glean, all the other Intelligence categories, as the ones to follow all connect with each other, and in some cases rely on each other. For CYBINT, it is no different as an example, the following disciplines overlap with CYBINT:

OSINT - public information about cyber characteristics of systems, such as IP address.

SOCMINT - information about the systems involved with social media. An example of this would be the location of Facebook servers.

HUMINT - information gathered form covert interactions with people in the know.

An example would be information collected at a conference.

TECHINT - this is where we would get the scientific and technical information about cyber equipment.

Out of CYBINT comes Cyber Security, which is the technologies, processes, and practices used to protect from cyber-attacks. The information Gathered via CYBINT is how we learn of these possible attacks, and the Cyber Security folks find the way to stop it.

There are 4 main types of CYBINT tools you need. Now keep in mind these tools also fall into other intelligence categories, but these tools will also provide alot of intelligence for CYBINT, and while doing so will also protect your system. These tools are also tools for anyone who has a computer should have and use. They will fall under both monitoring and prevention. They are:

Firewalls - this is the first line of defense against malware, viruses, spying, and other threats it looks at both incoming and outgoing traffic. Example of firewalls or firewall vendors are: Fortinet FortiGate, Cisco, SonicWall, Check Point, Microsoft, and 360 Security

Antivirus - this is software designed to stop the effect of viruses on a system. They do so by monitoring and preventing potential threats from even getting on the system, as well as monitoring what is already on the system for issues. Examples of Antivirus software are TOTALAV, Norton, AVG, AVAST, McAfee, and 360 Security.

Anti-Spyware Software - this is simply put software that helps to stop and monitor your system from spyware. Examples of Anti-Spyware software are Scanguard, Bitdefender, Bullguard, and Trend Micros.

Password Management Software - this software that helps save you time by keeping all your passwords easily accessible. It also, if it is a good one will help to secure your passwords within encrypted measures. Meaning whatever your password is, in the system you are using it is encrypted and there for much more secure. This is much more secure than saving your passwords in browsers and usually makes them more portable. Some examples are Lastpass, Dashlane, RoboForm, and Keeper.

Now there are some software packages out there that can do it all with regard to protecting your system. Examples are 360 Security, McAfee, Norton, and Microsoft.

Tools that might be used and will also be shown in other categories are:

WHOIS - displays information about a given site, IP address, etc.

FindSubdomain - this helps you find subdomains of main domains, as well as open ports, IP ports, certificates, and more.

Cryptcheck - this checks your domain for issues, and more.

Wireshark - packet sniffer tools, allows for monitoring of systems.

Nagios XI - network monitoring tools.

Chapter 19

IMPORTANT ANNOUNCEMENT

Now throughout the following chapters, we will talk about OSINT tools and methods. Alot of these will be familiar. OSINT tools can be rated by the level of the Web they work within (see Chapter 3 for Web levels). We as staffing professionals will typically only work in the L2, L1, and L0 part of the Web there for most of the tools we will discuss will be rated no deeper than L2. Level L3 and deeper are the places very few staffing professionals should go, and while I might mention a tool or 2 that can work there, I do so because they do something in the L0-L2 area as well that I think can be helpful, not so you can delve below L2.

Chapter 20

SOCMINT (Social Media Intelligence)

SOCMINT is a huge category. Alot of it will also fall under OSINT. In fact, SOCMINT is often called the wayward child of OSINT. SOCMINT is intelligence gathered from social media, specifically from the tools, and solutions that can be used to monitor social media in all its varying forms.

SOCMINT or the types of social media we would want comes in several forms:

Real Information - this is the stuff that is real and legit and does not have any secret stuff. Examples might be rating on Glassdoor, or LinkedIn followers.

Secure information - this is information that should not be being posted out on the web. Example might be login information, project reports, etc.

Disinformation - this is information that is incorrect. Now disinformation comes in two types. Accidental- meaning they did not know it was wrong. Purposeful-meaning they are doing it on purpose to confuse people, see the 2016 election for an example.

Potential uses of Social Media Intelligence:

Situational Awareness - developing an overview of an unknown but relevant situation.

Ongoing Monitoring - daily tracking of account activity and keywords.

Social Network Analysis - acquiring an understanding of the social dynamics for large scale data.

Priority Information Requests - getting answers to important questions, to make a decision.

Investigations - getting additional information on targets.

Engagement- analyzing information around social communications for the purpose of engagement.

Performance - assess performance of engagement techniques against a specific target.

Now how do we use it in staffing, well IT IS simple. We use SOCMINT to source; we use it to learn more about candidates, competitors, and our own company and competitors. When you go onto Facebook looking for candidates you are using SOCMINT to source. When you go onto AngelList to check out companies and such that is SOCMINT.

Now there are also other sub categories that fall under SOCMINT, while I am not going to go through every sub category I will go through one. Metadata, which as you saw in the definitions, is simply data about data. Now Metadata comes in several types:

Descriptive - provide title, subject, genre, author, and creation date.

Rights - this can include copyright, who owns the rights, and license terms.

Technical - this includes file types, size, creation date and time, type of compression and more.

Preservation - this is navigation data, such as where the item's place in the hierarchy or sequence.

Markup Language - this provides heading, name, date, list and paragraph. This is used or navigation and interoperability.

Now, let's look at some potential uses for SOCMINT:

Situational Awareness - finding info or an overview on a situation that you might feel is interesting. For staffing that might be a company saying they might be laying people off. A tool that can help you here is Owler.

Ongoing Monitoring - this is when you keep an eye on someone's profile or site. This can help when you find a profile but they say they are not looking. You can set an alert when they change their page and that could alert you when they are looking. A tool that can help you here is Google Alerts.

Social Network Analysis - this is where you look for data on a specific social media platform to better understand how users are using it and how you can. Example of this would have been in the early days of Github. Staffing professionals were not sure how to use it, but they kept watching it and learning until they figured it out. A tool that can help with this is Website Onepage Analyzer.

Priority Information Requests - This is on sites where you can ask important question to help you make a choice. Example of this is Quora. Of course, for us in staffing this is a gold mine. Example following a series of questions on java development, guess who the people asking and answering are? Java people that is who.

Investigations - this is basically acquiring additional information on a person or organization. For staffing that could be learning more about their background than what their LinkedIn profile might say or contact information. A tool than can help here is PIPL.

Engagement - this is where you analyze information and communications of someone with the goal to engage yourself. For staffing this could mean finding an email, learning enough about someone to write a personalized email. Tools that can help you with this include; Humantic, Precontact tool, and Swordfish.**

Performance - this is where you assess the progress and effectiveness of a given SOCMINT activity. An example for staffing might be analyzing the success of your outreach. Tools that can help with that are; Seekout, Hiretual, and other outreach tools that measure success.

To give you an idea just how important SOCMINT is, there is 2.5 quintillion (18 zeroes) of new data produced daily that is a great deal. Now keep in mind that does not mean you can access it all through the common/clearnet and surface web where most staffing professional work, however even within the surface web there is a ton. If as some experts say the surface/clearnet make sup between 1-5 percent of the total web that still means over 12.5 with 8 zeros, so there is still alot.

Social Media can take on different forms or categories. They can even fit into more than one category, however with all that said, here are some of the forms/categories and subcategories:

Social Networks - a site that allows users to interact. An example would be Facebook

Bookmarking sites - sites that allow you to share bookmarks and such. An example would be Stumbleupon.

Social News/Crowed Sourced Content - these are sites that allow users to post news links, and other crowd sourced content. An example might be Reddit.

Media Sharing - these are sites that allow you to share media. An example might be YouTube.

Microblogging/Micromedia - these are sites that allow for short written entries. An example is Twitter.

Blogs and Forums - these are conversational based sites that allow for full written communication. An example is Blogger.

SMS/Voice/Messaging - these are messaging sites or tools that allow for quick easy communication between people. An example would be WhatsApp, Skype or AIM.

Misc - forms of SOCMINT that don't fall under the other categories, an example might be GitHub.

Combined - these are sites that fit into more than one category. An example would be LinkedIn.

Interest and Curated Networks - these are networks that are interest specific and may curate info for that specific area. An example might be Netmoms.

Reputation - these are sites that have reputational information, maybe even a number system, this category is very closely related to the Review/Rating category but not exactly the same. As this category is more about a specific person than a company or product. An example might be WebMii.

Video - this category is obvious and easy. An example of this would be Vimeo.

Documents/Content - this is basically storage sites of varying kinds, usually related to some kind of document, an example would be Slideshare.

Gaming - like it says gaming social sites. An example would be Dragon Age.

Apps (mobile) - these are as the title suggest apps that are relevant to SOCMINT. An example would be Pocket.

Music - like the title suggest sites about music, where you can still gain some info on people. An example would be last.fm.

Wikis- we have all heard about the Wikis and obviously Wikipedia is an example.

Pictures - these are sites that are heavy picture orientated. An example is Pinterest.

Social Media Tools - this is a category of tools that can be used for social media but also provide an avenue for finding info. An example would be AddThis.

Review/Ratings sites - these are sites that allow for a rating or review. This differs from reputation in that this category is more about a product or company than an individual. An example would be Goodreads.

Question/Answer sites - these are sites designed around asking and answering questions, an example would be askmee.

Live Casting/Life Streams - this is an interesting category, as it says these are those live in real-time casting sites and or tools. An example would be Make.tv

Social Shopping/Commerce - these are sites that are related to shopping or commerce. Yes, you can use these to source. I mean if someone writes a book on Java, I bet they are a Java Developer. An example would be DailyDeal.

Collaboration - these are sites that allow for collaboration between people, even if they don't really know each other, An example might be Doodle.

Influence - this is another one related to others such as Review/Rating. However, with this one it is not people giving you the score it is a social media-based algorithm.

Location Based Services/sites - this is as it says sites and services that are primarily location orientated tools. This can help in staffing in that you can see where people are or go, and get a feel of their likes, conferences they attend etc. An example is Foursquare.

Now that we know the types of SOCMINT let's look at some specific sites.

Facebook - we all know this one, it is an untapped resource of information, and candidates with over 3.5 billion people on it, and a whopping 65 million companies using it to promote their business. There are tools a plenty that can help with sourcing on Facebook, and we will discuss some later in this chapter.

You Tube - with over 1.9 billion users, and plenty of ways to source this is a great site. For those that have been in a cave this is a video publishing site.

WhatsApp - boasting over 1.5 billion users, this app is growing strong, this app is a messaging app, that is very popular in over 180 countries. This app which originally was used for private messaging has since grown to be a business app.

WeChat - has 1.06 billion users and is another messaging app.

Instagram - with over 1 billion users this has been an up and coming site/app for a while. It allows for rich photo and video sharing.

LinkedIn - well they say they have over 6 million people. Keep in mind they also have alot of duplicate profiles, fake profiles, and other types of profiles that put into question just how many they really have. That said it is the top Business social site as of now. It has messaging capabilities and alot more. Some say it is more of a job board than a social site. However, it still falls under the category of Social...for now.

Twitter - who boasts 336+ million users and growing. It is a simple but effective messaging and micro blogging site. It allows for upload of links, videos, picture, and more.

Now of course there are alot more, below is a list of some of them with their monthly user numbers:

YouTube   1,900,000,000

Qzone   563,000,000

Weibo   376,000,000

Reddit   330,000,000

Pinterest	200,000,000
Ask.fm	160,000,000
Tumblr	115,000,000
Flickr	112,000,000
VK	97,000,000
Odnoklassniki	71,000,000
Meetup	35,300,000

Well we are at that point in this chapter where I talk tools. I will mention a few tools, and what they do that can help you with SOCMINT. The reason only a few is because alot of the tools that help you with SOCMINT also helps you with OSINT, since all of SOCMINT is also OSINT.

Tools:

API (see definition in definitions page) - these can be used in conjunction with say excel to find information, an example would be Block Spring.

Treeverse - this is a tool for visualizing and navigating Twitter conversation threads.

Binsearch - a usenet search.

Bulk Facebook ID finder - this finds Facebook IDs in bulk.

Omnisci - tweet map geo location.

Reddit Investigator - provide a Reddit name and get everything you need.

Geo find for YouTube - a tool that lets you use YouTube for location information.

GramFly - Instagram interaction search and reports.

Now one thing before we end. There is a thing called "Dark Social". Dark Social is a term used by marketers and the like to describe website referrals that are difficult to track. Dark Social traffic doesn't seem to have a specific source which makes it a challenge to monitor.

Well there you have it, SOCMINT in all its glory. I did not double star anything in this chapter as something I use as a preference. Due to the sheer number of categories and tools that work here, after all this category is all of Social Media. There will be more related to SOCMINT in the next chapter as we venture to the heart of this book OSINT.

Chapter 21

OSINT - Open Sources Intelligence

Open Source Intelligence (OSINT) is exactly what it sounds like, data collected from publicly available sources. This does not mean free, just publicly available. Despite what some say OSINT and research are related and sometimes by doing one you can be doing the other.

So first let's look at the history of OSINT. OSINT can trace its start all the way back to 1832 and the Foreign Broadcast Information Service. It played a large role in WW2 and has continued to develop into one of the primary intelligence tools. In fact, it is believed that up to 80% of the material analyst review (CIA, NSA, public and private), could be considered OSINT.

William Donovan, labeled by some as the father of OSINT, was a veteran who later became a lawyer, and thought these careers he had the opportunity to connect with one Franklin Delano Roosevelt (FDR), the man who one day would become President. This connection led to the creation of an intelligence agency in the US. This led to the creation of the Office of Strategic Services (OSS), this was the precursor to the CIA. Prior to this the US saw intelligence and spying as not gentlemanly and therefore did not participate.

The OSS had an entire division dedicated to OSINT; Though back in those days we are mainly talking media (see categories below). They looked at things like obituaries, general news- specifically foreign both in print and radio, and more.

After WW2 OSINT became a cornerstone of intelligence, with the government and military agencies staffing themselves with librarians and researchers whose sole job was to do OSINT. Shortly after this the world of OSINT went into hibernation. This did not change until 2009 when Iran was going through a revolution of shorts and millions took to the internet to flood it with information about major political events. This began the start of a series of events that leads us to today where OSINT is once again front and center in our intelligence world.

When thinking about OSINT it is good to realize that in alot of cases it is an investigation that prompts the use of OSINT. Now I know you thinking okay how does that connect to Staffing? Well if you have decided you need to find more information about a person, even if it is just emails you are technically starting an investigation into the person and the finding of that person information. This same concept can go for groups of people like say Java Developer, or even a specific company. OSINT is primarily used for law enforcement, national security, and business intelligence, of which Staffing would fall under. OSINT falls under 6 main categories of information flow:

Media - there is print type media such as newspapers, and magazines, radio media, and television all of which can be across and between countries. Examples of this kind of OSINT would be using a newspaper to research job adds to figure out what companies are looking and what they are looking for. Keep in mind while we are saying newspaper that does not mean it is hard copy this could be the newspaper as you see it on the web. An example tool you might use in this category is a simple boolean string to find data targeting a specific newspaper and x-raying in.

Internet - this is the biggest category and includes; online publications, blogs, discussion groups, most social media sites such as Facebook. This group also includes what is called citizen media, which includes; cell phone videos, and user created content.

Public Government Data - this is simply put public government reports, budgets, hearings, directories, press conferences, websites, and more. Even though the source is a government this is all publicly accessible information.

Professional and Academic Publications - this is information gathered from professional and academic journals, conferences, symposiums, papers, dissertations, theses, and the like.

Commercial Data - this is commercial imagery, financial, industrial assessments, and databases.

Grey Literature - this is technical reports, preprints, patents, working papers, white papers, business documents, unpublished works, newsletters and other documents.

Keep in mind the key part of OSINT is that it is open source. This means anyone and everyone has access to it, and in some cases access to change it. So that means we need to double check the information we get to ensure it is legitimate.

Given the size, use, and scope of OSINT today it is no surprise that there are organizations that specialize in OSINT. These include:

Open Source Center - this is a government led community where you can gain access to OSINT reporting and analysis.

BBC Monitoring - this is the department within the British Broadcasting Corporation that monitors the foreign media.

Janes Information Group - this is a British company founded in 1898 that specializes in the gathering of OSINT as it relates to; military, terrorism, state stability, serious and organized crime, proliferation and procurement intelligence, aerospace, and transportation subjects.

The Economist Intelligence Unit - this is the business intelligence, research, and analysis division of the British Economist Group.

Oxford Analytica - is a small OSINT firm and specializes in geopolitical and macroeconomic subjects.

Now of course there are more, and this list does not include groups or bodies where you can learn about OSINT or the tools you might use; though that is coming very soon.

OSINT can be of interest to different people or organizations. I will mention a few and why each would be interested. Keep in mind this is not all inclusive and there are others.

Government - this one is obvious the government and its many intelligence agencies would be one of the biggest users of OSINT.

International Organizations - these organizations include the UN (United Nations), and the Red Cross both of whom use OSINT for various reasons such as supporting peacekeeping and relief efforts during times of crisis or disaster.

Law Enforcement Agencies - Police and other Law agencies use OSINT to help with their investigations. I mean I am sure at some point you have watched an SVU (Law and Order Special Victims Unit) episode only to see them gain valuable information from a social media page.

Business Corporations - knowledge or information is power so it is no wonder a company would want as much as possible. This information can help with marketing, hiring, and much more. An example would be layoffs, and targeting a company that is reportedly having layoffs for staffing purposes. Companies will also look to use OSINT for other things that are not financially motivated. These can include ascertaining any data leaks, or vulnerabilities and to also create their own threat intelligence strategies.

Penetration Tester and Black Hat Hackers/Criminal Organizations - OSINT is a prime avenue for hackers and pen testers to gather information about a target.

Privacy-Conscious People - as it sounds these are just regular people who want to check how people on the outside can break into their system or check what the outside world sees about them.

Terrorist Organizations - simply put, you put out there you are going to a concert and there will be 10k+ people there. A terrorist group could use that to decide to target that concert.

Now the process of gathering this information that OSINT provides usually takes on one of three types:

Passive Collection - this is the most common information gathering type. It is also the easiest as it is simply finding the information that is already easily available, where no one would be aware that the collection is happening.

Semi-passive - this is a type of collection that would send some limited traffic to a specific server to gain general information. This traffic tries to resemble normal traffic so as not to attract any attention, but there is that chance, and as such is Semi-passive.

Active Collections - this type is where you interact directly with the systems to gather information and the target will more than likely catch on. Think of these 3 types of collection as a matter of being caught. Passive means not likely, semi-passive means semi likely and active means highly likely. Now of course there is more to it, but I am trying to keep it simple.

Now let's look at the principal benefits of using OSINT:

Less Risky - using Publicly available information to collect intelligence has little to no risk compared to other forms of intelligence such as HUMINT, where talking with someone always raises concern.

Cost Effective - generally OSINT is cost effective, I mean it cost nothing to have access to Facebook, Twitter, and others.

Ease of accessibility - OSINT resources are easily and readily available, there are 100s of social sites and more every day.

Legal Issues - most OSINT resources can be shared between people without worrying about legal or copyright issues.

Aiding financial investigators - OSINT can allow specialize agencies to detect tax evaders, such as companies, celebrities etc.

Fighting against online counterfeiting - OSINT can be key in finding false products, services and direct law enforcement to close the sites.

Maintaining national Security and political stability - OSINT can be used as a tool for influencing our political stability. A little dissemination of false information can impact how we vote, and by proxy impact our national security.

Now as with anything in life if there is a pro there must be a con, so the cons are:

Sheer volume of data - well there are 100s of social sites out there, 1000s of newspapers, and 100s of document repositories. While this does provide a huge treasure trove of information the sheer volume can also become a problem.

Reliability of sources - well this is simple you can't always rely on the information you get. Someone can put anything they want on their Facebook page. The Wikis are all crowd sourced so who knows how accurate the info is.

Human Efforts - this relates back to the sheer amount of data available and the fact that we have to go through it. Even using tools that are available it takes time and time is money.

So, let's look at some answers to questions you need to have in order to start using OSINT:

What am I looking for - you need to have an end game, what are you wanting to accomplish? For example; an email would be nice.

What is my main research - goal this relates to the first one, but instead of an email it is a verified email.

What or who is your target - think of this as the name of the person you are looking for.

How am I going to conduct my research: think of this as where will you start.

Now let's look at some of the most popular OSINT techniques, resources or things we do with OSINT, while keeping mind there will be some redundancy with these techniques:

- Collect employee full names, job roles, as well as technology they are using. For staffing this would be like creating an org chart or tech usage chart.
- Review and monitor search engine information. For staffing this would be like setting up a google alert to keep notified on things with a given company, person etc.
- Monitoring personal and corporate blogs and forums. This is like when staffing looks for indications of layoffs, or new products.
- Identify all social networks used by a target. This is like when staffing will look for the social footprint of a person or company.

- Review content available on social networks. Whereas the previous techniques were indemnifying social sites, here we review it looking for clues such as; what language do they program in.
- Usage of people data collection tools such as PIPL to find information on an entity. For staffing this would be getting an email.
- Accessing old cached data. For staffing this would be like using the Way back Time Machine (more on this later).
- Identifying mobile numbers, emails, landlines and other ways to contact a person or use for further research.
- Search for photographs or Videos -this stand for itself and in staffing might be using a Photo to find more info on someone.
- Use Google Maps or other such tools. This can result in locating an address, a pattern and more.
- Use tools to search DNS, Internet connected devices, and other places for additional information.

Now I know some of these seem more like categories than actual techniques or resources, but think of them as huge broad-based techniques. The thing to keep in mind for us in staffing is we should be touching on all of them and later in this book we will discuss the tools that can help you do just that.

For the purposes of this book we are mostly going to use the OSINT tools categories as outlined on the OSINT framework site but we will add a twist, and add one other category that I feel should be added. While some are redundant, most of these tools all align with the techniques, you just read about.

Now keep in mind we are not going to go into detail on all of these categories, as some are not relevant for staffing, sourcing, and recruiting. That said I will explain all of them to varying degrees, and hit hard the ones that matter to us most. We will of course list some tools, methods and or tips for each category. The categories that are relevant to Staffing will have ** next to them. We will also include a couple of surprises along the way, so read carefully.

These categories are:

Usernames** - these are things that we use when on the internet and performing social site related actions. However, usernames can also be a way for us to find things about the users to include their real names. Humans are creatures of habit. If they use a particular username on one site the odds are good, they use it on others. Also, if they use a particular user name alot there is a good chance they will have an email address using that username as the naming convention part of the email, meaning the part before the "@" part of the email. In addition, there is always the google way. Some of the tools that can help us with identifying where a username might be being used are:

Knowem - this is a site that allows you to enter a username and see every place it is being used. This can lead us to sites where it is being used that might be owned by the target and thereby provide more info.

Social Catfish - simply put this is another username lookup, but it also can allow you to look up names, emails, phone, and image searches.

Usersherlock - this tool has performed over 32 million searches and like the others looks to see where else the user name might have been used.

Namecheckr - this is another tool that also allows you to search based on username, however it also allows you to target a specific social site to search.

Email Address** - I am not going to insult you by telling you what an email address is. However, remember we are talking tools, methods and site and to that extent these are tools that can help use figure out work or personnel email addresses. For staffing this is one of the biggest, and most important categories of tools as we always need to be able to contact any person we find. It is estimated that 88% of people prefer their initial recruiting outreach to be via email. Also, an email can be your passport to finding more info about the person as you can research based on an email address. For us here in the US there are the 26-29 or so email domains that 98% of all people have an email with. (Keep in mind this category does not include sourcing tools that also have an email finding capability, those will be listed in another category) They are;

Gmail - free email domain owned by Google, also has a Google company capability however that is not free

Hotmail - the old Microsoft free mail domain, while you can't get emails with this domain any more those that have them can still use them.

Outlook - the new Microsoft free email domain taking the place of Hotmail.

Yahoo - this is an email services started in 1997 by Yahoo of course.

AOL - this was a web portal that can trace its lineage all the way back to the Commodore 64. It got started in 1985 and exists today and includes an email domain.

Lycos - is a web search engine and web portal that started in 1994. It spun out of Carnegie Mellon University and of course has an email service

MSN - Microsoft launched this web portal in 1995 and it is still going strong. Though you can't get an email with MSN anymore as it is all Outlook, you will still see some out there.

Excite - this is an internet portal that was launched in 1995. Like the others of course it has an email service

Comcast - I think everyone knows all about Comcast, and they all know it has an email service.

Me - this started as MobileMe and was a subscription-based service from Apple. It started as Itools, and then changed to MobileMe and is now Icloud, and includes an email service.

SBCGlobal/Bellsouth/ATT - was the mail service and domain from what was Southwestern Bell Corporation (SBC). When SBC merged with ATT the people with email where given the option to keep what they had or change to an ATT email. Same goes for Bellsouth.

Verizon - this was a separate email but has now been rolled into AOL however there are still Verizon emails out there.

Netzero - is an internet service provider that has been around since 1998 and has an email service.

Fastmail - is an email service offering both paid and free email accounts. It launched in 1999 and is based out of Australia

Mail.com - is an email service and web portal, that was launched in 1995, and its parent company is United Internet out of Germany.

Care2 - is a social networking website that was founded in 1998. It was designed to connect activists from around the world. Of course, it has an email service.

GMX - this is a free advertising-supported email service. It was launched in 1997 and has over 11 million users.

Gawab - is a free email service that was established in 1999.

Inbox - is an email service provider that supplies various security measures.

Earthlink - this is an IT security company that provides internet access, email, and web hosting services.

Cox - this is Cox Communications email service and may also be called webmail.

Zoho - this is a web based online office suite which includes an email service

BTinternet - this is an email service provider

Charter - this is Charter Communications email service

Protonmail - this is an end to end encrypted email service found in 2014 with over 10 million users.

Note almost all of these are free email providers.

Tools that we might use with regards to emails would include tools to find emails; research based on emails as well as validates emails. Some of these include by type:

Email Finders:

Swordfish** - a great resource it finds emails and phone number while in LinkedIn, Twitter and Facebook with more coming.

The Reach** - This is a great tool that provides contact info on such sites as LinkedIn, Facebook, AngelList and twitter.

Precontact tools** -A great tool that can find email and phone number while in Linkedin

Nymeria** - This tool finds contact info on LinkedIn

Adorito - this tool finds email address on LinkedIn

Kendo - this tool finds emails on LinkedIn

JobJet** - this tool finds emails and stuff on sites like LinkedIn, GitHub, and Angel List

Email Validators:

Zapinfo** - this tool is a scraper that also validates emails, finds emails, and creates Boolean strings. However, since there is no OSINT tool category for scraping or creating Boolean, we will list it here.

Email Checker - this is the site called Email Checker not the chrome ext. It allows the validating of emails one at a time.

Email Verifier online Domain Tools - this is a great tool; it allows for mass validation and also gives an in depth breaks down of why an email passes or fails.

Findemails - this tool not only can validate work or personnel emails, but can find you work emails in mass. IT does have a Chrome extension as well.

Email Based research - these are tools that can find you more info using an email:

Pipl - this tool can cross referenced people based on their email both work and personnel. It has a Chrome Extension that works well also.

Google/Bing/Other search engines - as you would expect if you have an email you can use any search engine to cross reference it and find more.

Seekout** - this is a sourcing tool, that can also allow you to upload a list of emails and it can enhance based on that email and find much more.

Facebook - this is a social site that if you put in an email in the search bar and it is the email, they used to sign up with it will match them up.

Domain Name** - this is the part of a network address that identifies it as belonging to a specific domain. It correlates to your website name which correlates to the URL. Now every webpage has a Url and that URL consists of 3 specific and main parts. This is a huge thing for staffing as this is what we use to x-ray. Below is a very simple breakdown.

Scheme: Also known as protocol, an example is HTTPs.

Domain name: This is the part that identifies a specific website you are trying to look at.

Path: This refers to everything after the domain.

How this can become useful is that when you own a domain it must be listed and If you don't pay extra that listing is public and always includes name, address, email and phone number of the owner. Which means unless you paid to hide it that info can be found. It is estimated 80% of people don't pay extra. Tools that help here include:

WHOIS** - this is an internet service that is used to look up information about a domain. Some of the information you might find is -domain name, the register, when it was registered, when it expires when it was updated, server names, and the registration contact, Administrative contact, and technical contact as well as raw information. There are various tools that can provide you this information, such as the Chrome extension IP Whois.

The following list of tools can help you find more information base don a URL:

Find Subdomains - this tool helps to find subdomains of the main domain; an example would be finding subdomains of microsoft.com where there might be a list of people who work there.

Images/Videos/Docs** - this category is simple as it is tools that can help us find or provide more info on Images, Videos or documents. For staffing that could mean Resumes, CVs, Bios, Profiles etc.

ImgOps - this tool lets you put in the url of an image and then see where else this image is being used, any effects being used, and much more.

TubeChop - this tool allows you to take the URL of a YouTube video and chop in up into sections.

Insecam - this tool allows you to see live public video cams from all over the world.

Social Networks** - these are networks of social interactions and personnel relationships. The chapter on SOCMINT also covered this. For staffing these are simple profiles, Bios, data about possible candidates and more. There are 100s of them I will only cover 3 of the more prevalent ones.

Facebook - this is one of the largest social sites with over 3.2 billion people.

Twitter -this is a free microblogging site.

Tweetreach - this is a tool that can give us analytics on a given twitter account.

Twitter List Search** - this is a site that allows you to find people who are part of lists, an example would be java developers.

Linkedin - is a professional social site that boasts over 600 million users.

Lisearcher - this is a LinkedIn x-raying tool.

LinkedinExport - this tool allows you to export your LinkedIn connections with emails.

Instant Messaging** - this is often shortened to IM and is the near real time exchange of messages via software. For staffing this is a way to communicate with people and even find out more about them. There are many of these such services, I will only cover a couple.

Skype - this is Microsoft instant messaging app.

Skype Resolver - this tool allows you to get the IP Address of a skype account

Skype2Email - this too lets you find emails connected to a skype User.

Snapchat - this is a mobile messaging app.

Somesnapcode - this site allows you to search snapchat user names by categories.

People Search Engines/tools** - these are tools and sites that can help you search for people and information on those people. For staffing it is self-evident how important this category is. Be prepared to put on our detective hat with this group. This is also perhaps the most used category within staffing.

Pipl - this is a search engines design specifically to find people. You can search by name, address, phone or email.

Radaris - this is a public records deep search tool.

TruePeopleSearch - this is a free people search engine that can provide alot of great information.

JohnDoe - this is another people search tool/site that can use a name, reverse phone or address to find people

Dating** - these are web-based sites that center around helping people find people for the end game of dating. For staffing these sites can sometimes provide some great information. The best tool for searching this site is the IntelTechniques Dating site Custom Search Engine. The top 5 sites are:

Match - this site was started in 1995, and has about 35 million unique monthly users.

Zoosk - this site started in 2011 and has about 11.5 million unique monthly users.

OkCupid - this site was started in 2004, has about 10 million monthly unique monthly users.

eHarmony - this site was started in 2000 and has about 7.1 million unique monthly users.

Badoo - this site was started in 2006 and has about 6 million unique monthly users.

Telephone numbers** - this is obviously the finding and validating of telephone numbers both cell and landline. Again, why this is important to staffing is obvious. This would also include Voicemail.

Slydial - this tool allows you to leave a voice mail without even calling the number.

SpyDialer - this tool has a free reverse phone number look up.

Phone Validator - this tool allows you to look up and see if it is a landline or cell phone.

Swordfish** - this tool finds phone numbers on when use don various social sites.

Public Records** - this is as it sounds, information you can find form public resources. For staffing these can find information about a candidate.

Property Records - this is information that can be found form property records that exist for all public and private property.

Homerty - this site allows you to enter an address, and you can see the owners and in most cases phone numbers and other information.

Court/Criminal Records - obviously this is as it sounds, not explanation is really needed.

MugShots - this site allows you to see mugshots and other info relevant info as it relates to people with Arrest records.

Government Records - this is data or information that can be found from government records.

Federal Election Commission (FEC)** - this is a great site full of government records on election contributions. However, this site allows you to search and the info you get back include full name, work title, company and address. More than enough to get what is needed to reach out.

Financial / Tax Records - also as it says these are financial and tax records of individuals or groups.

NETR Online - this site provides a host of public data to include some tac and financial data.

Birth Records - these are records related to the birth of someone or a group.

OnlineSearches -this site allows you to find the birthday records and more.

Death Records - these are records related to the death of someone.

SearchSystems.net - a site where you can find death records

Business Records** - this category covers alot of things; product development info, employee data, financial data and more. For staffing this might include payoff notices, contact info, competitor information and more.

AnnualReports - this site can provide annual reports for most companies.

Sec.Gov (EDGAR) - this site can provide a large amount of information on a company that is kept by the Security and Exchange commission (SEC).

OpenCorporates - another site that houses a treasure trove of information on over 169 million companies worldwide.

MarketVisual - this site lets you search professionals by name, company or title.

Geolocation Tools/Maps** - this category is as it says maps and other Geolocation tools. For staffing this can include information to help a candidate decide about relocation and much more.

Google Maps - this is Googles map product.

Dual Maps - this tool is a great high-end mapping tool, that combines Google Maps, Aerial Imagery, and Google Street View into one.

Earth Explorer - this tool is a mapping toll that can find anything on Earth. It allows for address search, date and time stamp, and more.

Search Engines (SE)** - I believe everyone knows what this category is and for staffing it is the backbone to sourcing. That said there are sub categories listed below with tools:

General Search - these are the most used and known and include such SE as the below:

Google - this is the largest and most used SE out there.

Bing - this is Microsoft's competitor to Google.

Bing vs. Google -this is a great site that allows you to run the same search in both Google and Bing and see the difference in the results.

ISearchFrom - this is a special SE that searches Google for results but allows you to easily pick Country, Language, or Device to use in your searching. So, you could decide to search like you're in England, in German and using an Android device.

Meta Search - these are search engines that search multiple SEs at one time.

Iseek - this is an academic SE that searches many SEs to bring back its results.

Carrot2 - this tool is an open source clustering SE. It searched many other SEs and also provides some other rather interesting capabilities.

SearX - this is a prototypical Meta Search engine.

Code Search - these tools allow you to search for code or in code repositories.

SearchCode - this tool searches over 20 billion lines of code form over 7 million projects. It searches such sites as; Bitbucket, Github, Google Code, Gitlab, and many others.

FTP (File Transfer Protocol) Search - these tool search FTPs.

GlobalFileSearch - this site allows you to search public FTP page and sites.

Academic/Publication Search - these tools search academia and publication such as white papers, patents etc.

Google Scholar - this is Googles academia search tool.

News Search - these tools that search for local, and world news.

PressReader - this tool brings you all kinds of news in any language form any country.

Other Search -these are tools that don't fit into the other categories.

SimilarSites - this tool helps you find sites that are similar to the one you are on or looking at.

Colossus International Search - this is a tool that, wait for it, lets you search for search engines all over the world.

Targeted Search Tools - these tools do very specific things that are slightly different form most SEs.

Million Short - this too allows you to ignore a specific number of the top results based on SEO. That means ignore say the top 1k results and see the next batch. This the only real way to see all the results in a google searches.

Google Custom Search Engine (CSE) - this is the tool that allows you to create a targeted custom search engine

Fact Checking - these are tools specifically designed for checking facts, originality etc.

FactCheck.org - this site lets you check the validity of questions and answers you see out in the social and news sphere.

Forums/Blogs/IRC (internet Relay Chat)** - this category are tools that let you search for Forums, Blogs etc. For staffing it is an eye into things about a candidate you might not find in other places as well as a chance to find candidates you might not find other places.

Omgili - this tool allows you to search Forums and such for information.

BlogSearchEngine - this tool as it the title says searches Blogs.

Blog-Search - this tool also searches for blog posting.

IRC Search - this tool searched chat rooms.

Archives** - these tools are tools that allow you to search older internet pages that have been put into archives. This is a great way for staffing to find things that might be available any more. It is sort of like a list of conference attendees that is no long republic but was at some point. There are 4 sub categories they are with tools:

Wayback Time Machine - this tool takes intermittent snap shots of the web and maintains a searchable archive.

Data Leaks - these are as they say archived leaked data.

WikiLeaks - I think we all know what this is, just in case remember the 2016 election?

Public Datasets -these are public sets of archived data.

VisualGenome - this is a tool that is a dataset of images that are being structured in such a way as to allow for connection mapping.

Other Media - this is media not included in the other categories.

Library of Congress - this is a site that has a huge searchable collection of newspapers and magazines from as far back as 1836.

Language Translation** - these are tools that can translate text and pictures to text as well as do analysis. For staffing this means being able to read a resume written in another language which if you need someone who speaks and writes another language can come in handy.

Text - tools that translates text to and from English.

DeepL - this is a site where you can paste in large section of text and choose the language it is in and to translate to.

Google & Bing - both of the top two search engines have translation capabilities of course.

FreeTranslation - this site is really good for large scale translation project, like whole books and such.

Pictures - these tools and sites can translate words in pictures to normal text.

Online OCR - this is an online tool that actually takes PDFs both text and pictures and changes them to a fully editable file.

Free Online OCR - this tool converts the text in any picture format to usable, editable text.

Analysis - These tools analyze text and pictures to gather information and insights.

Personality Insights -this tool takes the text written by someone to include from social media and gives you insights to their personality traits.

Humantic (formally Deep Sense)** - this tool uses social media profiles and multiple personality trait measuring methods to provide insights into to someone, to include recommendation for methods to contact them.

Metadata** - these are tools that can help you find and look at metadata. As it relates to staffing you can get information such as; author, date created, date modified, size, and more.

FOCO - this tool is a heavy OSINT tool; it can find metadata and other hidden data in virtually any document, picture or other media

Mobile Emulation** - these tools allow you to emulator specific mobile environments from your desktop. For staffing that means using mobile apps ion your desktop allowing you to use more in depth OSINT tools that are desktop dependent.

NoxPlayer - this is one of the best Android emulators there is and runs on Windows.

ElectricPlum - this tool is an Iphone, IPad, IOS development platform that emulates those devices on a Windows machine

Genealogical** - these are sites and tool that allow you to trace your genealogy. For staffing that can also mean contact information.

GenealogyInTime - this site is a CSE created to search nearly all Genealogy sites.

GenealogicReview - this is another Genealogy site that like the other can lead to contact info.

Classifieds** - these are small advertisements that are places in newspapers, sites and the like. How it relates to staffing is fairly simple if someone is selling a book on Java development and they are the author they are probably a java person.

Craigslist - this is perhaps the best-known site of its kind, and guess what there are people looking for jobs on their and they have resumes.

Documentation** - now I know what your, thinking documentation? We already had a category really close to this. This category is about collecting documentation and stuff for your investigation or search. For staffing it is collecting pieces of a puzzle that later becomes a candidate or way to contact a candidate.

Web Browsing - tools that can help you save information from web pages.

Zapinfo** - this is a great scraping tool that can scrape information from a web page, enhance it and have it available for export. An example might be a list of developers from Facebook.

Screen Capture - these tools capture an entire screen.

ShareX - this tool allows you to do full screen capture, file sharing and much more.

Map Location - this too allows you to get map location that are downloadable.

Batchgeo - this tool allows you to enter many or a single location and then maps it out and save it.

IP Address - this is a unique number which identifies each computer using the Internet Protocol to communicate over a network. These also provide location information which allows you access to certain pages. Also, if you look at the email header of a given email you can see the IP address of the computer it was sent from.

Infosniper - this tool allows you to see the location of a given IP address.

Utrace - like info sniper this to shows you the location of a given IP ADDRESS.

Transportation - this relates to vehicle, air traffic, marine and railway. There is no staffing use.

Reverse Genie - this tool allows you to look up info of a vehicle based on plate number, you can also do searches on phone, email, address, IP, Domain, and more.

Flightaware - live flight tracking, for nay flight, any location

Worldwide.Vessel Tracker - this can track any vessel any place in the globe.

Openrailwaymap - this is a tool that can show every railway track, signals, speeds and movement worldwide.

N2YO.com - satellite tracking tool that lets you see location, and launching of Satellite worldwide.

Terrorism - I think this is also category is obvious, and there is no Staffing use.

Global Terrorism Database (GTD) - this is a database that can provide alot of information as it relates to Terrorism.

Dark Web - this is the part of the web you don't want to go to.

Hunchly - this is a site that provides a daily report on the Dark Web.

Hidden Wiki – this is a site with links to Wiki.onion URLs and more.

Digital Currency - this is that list of mythical currency.

Bitcoin - the most well-known of the Digital Currencies.

Encoding/Decoding - This is a category with Encoding which is converting things to a particular form, and Decoding which means taking things from a form that is not readable by a human and making it readable for a human.

BarCode Reader - this is a tool that can read a bar code to get all the info behind it.

Malicious File Analysis - this is a category of tools than can find and analyze malicious files.

Hybrid Analysis - this tool is a simple and quick tool to analyze an object for malware.

Exploits & Advisories - these are typically databases of exploits that have been discovered.

Exploit Database - a simple but very robust database of found exploits.

Threat Intelligence - these are tools that analyze the potential threat of an object.

BotScout - a tool that helps identify and stop bots.

OpSec - This stands for Operational Security and is the process of identifying critical information.

Proxy Checker - this tool helps to check the security of a proxy.

Chapter 22

HUMINT - Human Intelligence

HUMINT (Human Intelligence) - is intelligence gathered from a person in a specific location.

examples include:

Espionage - which is also called spying and is the act of obtaining secure information without the permission of the person, or entity that holds it.

Friendly Accredited Diplomats - gaining information from Diplomats both ours and others.

Military Attaches - These are military experts who are attached to a diplomatic mission.

Non-governmental Organizations (NGO) - these are usually nonprofit but sometimes are also international organizations. These are generally involved with humanitarian, Health care, education, social and human rights, and other such functions

Patrols- these are both military and civilian patrolling duties related to standard military or police type tactics.

Prisoner of War (POW) - we are talking precisely what it says prisoners of war or detainees who might have heard something of interest.

Refugees - these are generally displaced people who have been forced to leave their homes and may have some valuable information.

With regards to these types of HUMINT, there is little in the ways of tools, as this involves actual speaking to people. Now, this speaking can be done over various communications, such as SMS, Phone, Video, etc. As such, there are some tools that can hellp. Also, as it relates to recruiting, staffing, or sourcing, this is where the ability to communicate is essential. In fact, when you get someone to talk and provide information, it is sometimes called recruiting or interviewing.

Now usually I would try to provide some examples of tools and such but, most fall under SOCMINT which you read about earlier. There are support tools, main tools for gathering your info, and notes from conversations. With that being the case, I would say tools like MS Office, Google Docs, any translation software, in the case of sourcing it would include any phone or in person interviewing documents, forms, etc. Also, there are video and other communication tools that can be used for staffing, such as:

Loom - a video interviewing system
Skype - a communication program **
Zoom - a conferencing tool **
Uber - a conferencing tool **
Sparkhire - video interviewing
Hirevue - video interviewing tool

While there is not alot in the ways of tools, as it relates to staffing and HUMINT, there are methodologies that apply. Any interviewing method, procedures would apply here, for example:

Behavioral Interviewing- this is an interview technique designed to assess candidates based on past actions and behaviors.

Lookology - Lookology is the advanced art of utilizing nonverbal communication in interviewing, sales meetings, and more.

Lisology - is the art of not just hearing what is said but listening to what it meant, how it is said, the words used, the way they are put together to form answers or phrases, the inflection in peoples voices, the stutters, the silence, the emotion or lack thereof behind what is said, what is not said and more. Think of it as "Active Listening" on steroids.

Looklisology - the combination of Lookology and Lisology

BTOS Interviewing System - the premise behind the BTOS (Business, Targeted, Open Door, and Sequential Interviewing system) is utilizing behavioral interviewing and Looklisology (see the previous blog posting on Looklisology) and Probing questioning to combine and form a unique, highly flexible, and successful interviewing system. To start let's look at the definitions of each of the main parts of BTOS;

Business Behavioral Interviewing (BBI) - Business Behavioral interviewing has a specific style and approach. This approach relies on the use of open-ended questions versus closed questions that require a simple yes or no answer. Business Behavioral Questions provide interviewers with a pattern of behavior, business/soft skills (negotiating skills, problem-solving, communication, etc..), evidence to judge a candidate's ability to perform within the company's culture and general business style and approach. Most of these falls under general skills that most employees should have, regardless of job function. You can also use this type of interviewing question to assess fit within a group or organization.

Targeted Behavioral Interviewing (TBI) - Targeted Behavioral Interviewing style questions that are geared toward technical/specific job/function skill areas, "Tell me about a time you had to design a website?" of course, out of this, you will move into Open Door and Sequential interviewing. Remember the whole BTOS system is connected. One thing will always lead to another.

Open Door Interviewing - this is where your utilization of your Looklisology skills, pay off the most, in noticing parts of an answer to a question that should be probed further i.e., you ask a question about an uncomfortable situation, and you see when giving a part of the answer the person seems to get nervous. This opens the door for you to probe further all the while doing so, utilizing a BBI, TBI, or Probing Style.

Sequential Interviewing - this is simply when you take the next logical step in questioning anyone. Example if you ask them to tell you a time when they had to build a website, one of the following questions to ask in the sequence might be, what tools, languages, etc. did you use. These next questions do not have to be TBI or BBI type questions but more of the Probing Style.

Probing style interview questions - these styles of questions are much more direct and not behaviorally based at all.

These questions are used primarily in Open Door or Sequential interviewing. These questions are designed to get specific information from a person i.e., "What tools did you use in designing the website." This Style can be used on technical skills, general business skills, and at any time where you need a specific non-behaviorally based answer.

More on all the afore mentioned methods can be found in my first book "Staffing Da Costa Style"

Another function within staffing that could fall under HUMINT is the initial outreach. With regards to initial outreach, this can be via, phone, text, or email. For our purposes, we will talk about email, given 88% of all candidates prefer email as the initial outreach. Now with regards to emails, there are 4 parts to an email; the subject, the introduction, the body, and the closing/signature block. We will focus on the subject and body as the other 2 tend to be fairly standard. We all know the name of the game is personalization, and for that, there are alot of tools that can help us.

The Subject line is the first thing they see, 45% of all emails are opened based on the subject. Studies show that for max reply rate you want to keep it to 30 or fewer characters. Some tools can help you with this, they are:

Subject Line Tester - this is a site that grades your subject based on numerous data points, to see what the attention score is, that meaning how likely is that subject line to grab someone's attention and thus lead to being opened.

Textio - this tool will not only tell you how good the Subject line is but the whole email.

The body is the meat and potatoes of the email. When writing this, you should think of "What's in it for Me" (WIFM), and remember by me we mean the candidate. Some things to take into account when writing your email;

Sizzle - be different; do go with the same old we have a job for your stuff.

Have Style - be warm, not creepy, but real while maintaining any boundaries of decorum.

Call to action - have a specific call to action for either replying by the candidate or follow up by you

Ensure your signature block is there - well without this you are limiting the ways for the candidate to reply other than email reply. Also helps validate who you are.

Tools that can help you are:

Textio - as stated already enables you to write a good email that is compelling by telling you the score of the email you wrote and making recommendations on how to make it better. **

Readability Score - this tool lets you know what grade level the email you wrote is at. It calculates it for both live reading and auto-reading by things like Alexa. The ideal is the 8th grade for life, the main reason is alot of people read on the go, and anything higher is harder to read, so they either wait or don't bother. Of course, if they wait the odds go down, they will ever read it. For auto-reading, the ideal is a 6th-grade level. **

Mosaic Track AI - this tool can tell you the engagement level of the email you wrote.**

Joblint - this tool lets you know if there are any cultural, realism, sexism issues with your email; in other words, things that might offend someone.**

Spam Check -this tool lets you know the spam score of your email. The lower the score, the less likely it will get caught in spam filters, which is one of the most significant issues with emails.**

Humantic - this tool gives you insights into the things that motivate your target, and examples of how best to communicate with them.**

A/B Testing - this is not really a tool so much as a methodology where by you get 2 highly rated subject lines, and 2 highly rated emails using the tools above. Then you mix and match sending 5 of each combination out and keep track of open rates, reply rates, etc. So, what we mean is 2 subject lines called s1 and s2. Two emails called E1 and E2. You then make the combinations which will be S1 and E1, S1 and E2, S2 and E1 and S2 and E2. Then send each of the 4 combinations to 5 people each and analyze the results to see which worked best.**

So, there you have it, tools, techniques, and processes, methodologies that can help you with HUMINT and staffing.

Chapter 23

SpiderFoot

Spiderfoot is an automation OSINT tool that can help find alot of information about someone. It searches over 100 public data sources to gather information to include; domain, IP addresses, emails, names, and more. It can run on Linux or Windows and has some great visuals. It is free and has full documentation making it easy to install and use. They also update it with new modules and capabilities regularly.

To download the tool, go to Spiderfoot and follow the directions for Linux or Windows. I will explain the installation form Windows below.

First, download the file to your computer. Then unzip into a directory. Once this is done to start the program, simply click on the sf.exe file in the Spiderfoot directory. A dialogue box will open, and the program will open. In the dialogue box, there will be a URL. You must copy this URL and paste it into a browser. Once there, you will see the Spiderfoot page. The first thing to do is go to settings and add in any APIs that are required, the documentation shows you how to do this is an easy way. To start a new scan simply press "New Scan," then give it a name, then add in the target. Your choices for a target are; Domain Name, IP Address, Host Name/Sub-domain, Subnet, email. Once this is done you can decide what info you want, I just use the All category. Then press "Run Scan."

What you will get is;

Status - you will see how much info it found and what category it fits into, meaning email, names, web content, User Accounts on External Sites, etc. This is in a chart type of presentation. You can hover over any of them and see how much it found. If you click on, then you will see what they found.

Browse -this is where you see the same data as above but in a pure text presentation.

Graph -this is where you see the data in a spider web presentation like what you might see in a criminal investigation with lines going from one piece of info to another.

Scan Settings -this is where you see what all the settings for the scan where and where the search went.

Log -this is where you see what if any issues there where with your scan. In most cases, you will only need the Status or Browse section, as you can see everything you need there. Email Addresses, social sites, and more. Simply click on what specifically you want, such as "Code Repository," and you will see if they have a code repository and the URL.

The sections that interest me the most, and I am sure will interest you are; Email, and External Site.

Spiderfoot has a new version called Spiderfoot HX which is a web-based version you can use right in your browser as well.

The HX version actually provides you with a little more information, however also requires you get alot more APIs.
Information on it can be found on the same page as the regular version of Spiderfoot.

Chapter 24

Creepy

Creepy is a Geolocation OSINT tool that allows you to gain OSINT information from the GEO tag of posts made on specific social networks. It shows the information on a map, allows filtering, based on the exact location, date as well as the ability to export to CSV. It can be run on Windows, Debian based OSs, Kali Linux, OSX and others. The instruction for installing and configuration is simple and listed on the download page. I will go through it for Windows below:

Simply download and run the installers and you are done. Once installed you click on Edit - Plugins Configuration and follow the instructions.

To use simply create a project by clicking New Project in Creepy. Then search for the target utilizing available plugins, which include:

Flickr - picture based Social Media.

Instagram - another Social Site.

Twitter - large microblogging site.

Once the search is done merely right click on the project and click analyze project and all will be revealed.

Now some are probably wondering okay, great, but how does that help me? How it helps is it can allow you to see the geo patterns of people. You might notice that not only the target person but others like that target such as say testers, all go to one place on say a Thursday. Because it is geo-based, you get to see the exact location which if it means a bar, you now know that they all go to that bar every Thursday after work. So, you can remember to go there and strike up a conversation, and away you go. FYI that is a truestory, and my friend who I helped figure this out ended up hiring 3 of the 5 he met there.

Chapter 25

HTTrack Website Copier

HTTrack is a free OSINT tool that allows you to download a website to your local directory. This includes images, documents, lists, and pretty much any file. Now, as you can imagine, it can take a long, long time, depending on the size of the site.

It can be run on Windows, Android and numerous versions of Linux to include; Debeian, Ubantu, and Gentoo. It can also be run on OSX, Fedora, and FreeBSD.

Installation is simple just download the Software and install. Below I will go over how to use it:

First, you choose a project name and destination folder by clicking the file and the new project. Then you add the URL you are targeting. Then click next, and then finish and away you go. Now there are some setting you will see as you run through this. However, most can be left as is and require no changes. Once the mirroring is downloaded, you can go to the destination folder and see the whole website.

Now how does this help us in staffing? Let's say you find a website that lists alot of the people who are involved with the site or company. You know contact info is there but requires alot of clicks to get to. With this tool, you can download the whole site and the offline use of other tools to gather all the info into a friendly usable format. FYI, I did this on a company site and came away with almost 20k people who worked there with contact info.

Chapter 26

OSIRT

OSIRT stands for "Open Source Internet Research Tool," and is a complete all in one, OSINT research environment. It is a Windows-based tool that was written in C #. It can run on Windows 7 and higher. This tool was created for law enforcement investigations, as it allows you to save everything you have on a target into projects. What makes this tool so good is what you can do within it; see below for some of its abilities:

Enhanced Web browsing - it looks and acts just like a browser you commonly used; the only difference is nothing touches the cloud.

Capture the Web - OSIRT has built-in tools for screen capturing, video capturing, and more.

Report Generation - once you have finished an investigation, you can download a helpful report with everything you found and how and where you found it.

TODo List - this is a simple to do list to remind you where you still need to search.

Of course, there are tools within this environment to include;

Whois - see previous chapters

DuckDuckGo - see previous chapters

Premade "user Agents" - to search specific sites

TOR - as you know TOR is your gateway to the Deep and Dark Web and comes built-in with OSIRT.

Installing OSIRT is very easy. You simply go to the OSIRT page and Download the installation file and install it. Next, you ensure you have "NET Framework 4.6.1 or higher as well as Visual C++. You will have to restart your computer, and then you are ready to go.

To start OSIRT, simply click the exe. file. When it first opens, you will get a page that gives you the option to Create a New Case, load an existing case, or view the audit log.

You will also see in the bottom right-hand corner the TOR button.

So, to start a new case, you click the new case button and then fill out the needed info, name, etc., and away you go. I will not go into more detail here, but the documentation and manuals are on the site and very easy to read and understand.

Now, of course, how does this help us in staffing? Simply put, when we in staffing do research on a person, or a company there is alot that goes into it, sometimes it is hard to remember all we did, and even harder to keep what we find organized. This tool allows us to do this and gives us numerous tools to help us.

Chapter 27

Maltego

Maltego is the GOLD standard for OSINT tools. It comes with the ability to do so much and provide so much that it can be the only tool you need.

Maltego has several versions:

Maltego XL -This is the premiere version of Maltego, provides all the capabilities of the tool but with enhanced ability to work with big data points while making a graphic of the data.

Maltego Classic -This version comes with all the functionality of the XL except the ability graphically handle large data points.

Maltego Ce -This is the version I recommend for staffing, for one, it is free, and while it does not have all the functions of the other two, it has more than enough. This is also the version I will be speaking about for the rest of this chapter.

When you see ** next to anything from this point on, that means this is a place for staffing.

Maltego can be used to find data relevant to the following Main categories of information:

People - names, email addresses, phone, aliases, social sites. What this means is you cans search under the people category and get all the info mentioned, using the information mentioned, so you can use a name and get emails, phone, aliases, and social sites. **

Groups - you can guess this is a category to find groups of people such as a Facebook group. **

Companies - as it states, this category allows you to gain info on companies. This can include; emails, sites, employee lists, documents, and more. **

Web Sites - this category would allow you to gain information on a website; it is such as; Owner, subsites, documents, and more. **

Internet Infrastructure - this category can find your info such as Domains, DNS names, Netblocks, and IP Addresses.

Affiliations - this is to see if you have an association with a group. This is not a category I recommend you play with as these groups include things like gangs and the like.

Documents and Files - as it sounds finding documents. **

Now while that is the type of data you can find, when using the tool, you will see the following choices of how to search for the type of data you need. These are called Entity Palettes and are very self-explanatory and include:

Events - under this, you will see conventions, conversations, incidents, meetings (business), meetings (social). **

Groups - under this, you will see Company, Education Institution, gang,

Online Group, Organizations, Political Movement, Religious. **

Infrastructure - Internet Autonomous System, Banner, DNS Name, Domain, IP Address, MX Record, NS Record, Netblock, URL, Tracking Code, Website. A category we don't need to really play in.

Location - airport, church, circular area, city, country, crime scene, GPS, harbor, home, office, prison, region, shop, train station, country.

Malware - hash, we don't need to really play in.

Passive Total - component, SSI certificate, tag, SSL expiration date, SSL fingerprint, SSI issue date, and more but this is a place we as staffing professionals don't need to go.

Penetration Testing - another category we don't need to really play in.

People - this is the main category we need to be in, however, even in this category, there are areas we don't need to touch. That said this category includes; business leader, employee, and numerous other, most of which are not relevant for staffing. **

Cryptocurrency - this is as it says. A category we don't need to really play in.

Personal - another category we play in big time. It includes; company, RSS feed, Alias, document, email address, Image, person, phone number, phrase, sentiment, organization. There are others, but these are the biggies. **

Devices - a category we don't need to really play in.

Social Network - as it says Social Networks.**

TMDB - this is movie stuff. A category we don't need to really play in.

Threat Grid - security threats. A category we don't need to really play in.

Tracking - this is a category where you will see things like; passport, Bank Account. A category we don't need to really play in.

Transportation - is what it sounds like. A category we don't need to really play in.

Weapons - again are what it sounds like. A category we don't need to really play in.

PeopleMon - this is an area we should play in. It includes; Email, Phone, Social Links, and more. **

Social Links - this is also as it sounds Social Media links and an area, we should play in. **

Now I know this is alot, but guess what? They have a recently used category that is always on top, so if you have specific things you use, they will always be right at the top of the lists.

Matlego can run on Windows, Mac, or Linux. It is easy to install. On Windows simply download the installation file, chose the OS and filetype and run it, and follow the directions. The rest is pretty easy, and the documentation on it is outstanding.

As it relates to staffing, it is pretty simple. You can't hide from this tool. My brother had a company that he sold back in the 80s. He wiped everything on it from the web. He then bet me I could not find much if anything on it. Needless to say, I used Maltego, and by the time I was done, I had the website, a list of his employees, emails, phone, etc. and my brother owed me a beer.

Chapter 28

Buscador

Buscador is an OSINT Linux based tool that works within a Virtual Machine environment. Think of this as a complete OSINT environment that can do virtually anything.

Let us start with the fact it works in a Virtual Machine, meaning security ready. Then add it has a built-in VPN so even more secure. Then finally add in it has TOR so it has all 3 of the biggies and is about as safe as you can get.

Now let's talk tools. The following is a list of tools that come with Buscador, installed, and ready to go:

Maltego - see chapter 27.

Spiderfoot - see chapter 23

Creepy - see chapter 24

HTTrack - see chapter 25

Custom Firefox browser and add-ons - designed for OSINT

Custom Chrome browser and add-ons - again created for OSINT

Tor Browser - see chapter 4

EmailHarvester - a tool that scrapes emails from websites.

And at least 20+ more OSINT tools. Now, of course, installing it. First, you must have a Virtual Machine, so see chapter 6. The instructions for how to install it are straightforward and listed on the website if you follow them, you will have no problems. They do have updates which will be listed on the website. Of course, each tool will also have updates, so you will need to use the update tools located in the settings area. There are alot of videos on YouTube on how to install and use this, so I recommend you watch them. Also, you can add more tools, extensions, etc.

Now the inevitable story of how about how I used this tool. Well I mean do I really need one? This tool can do it all, and anything you can do in any browser can be done in this tool and much much more, but much more securely. That said about a year ago I had found a forum where alot of developers where hanging out. I wanted to find everyone on it, their emails, names etc. Utilizing the tools that come in Buscador, I was able to do just that and ended up with almost 5k developers, their names, emails, places of work and titles.

https://inteltechniques.com/buscador/

Chapter 29

Sourcing Tool Supersets

These are my minimum go to tools, meaning while there are more I like, these are the minimum must haves and my first go to tools.

US:

Sourcing: Seekout, Hiretual, EngageTalent, Human Predictions, Amazing Hiring, Prophet, Rockstar Finder

International:

Sourcing: Seekout, Hiretual, Whoknows, Amazing Hiring, Human Predictions, Prophet, Rockstar Finder

Both:

Boolean: Source hub, SourcingLab, Sociallist, Zapinfo

Enhancing: Swordfish, Zapinfo, JobJet, Nymeria, Advanced Background Check, Truepeoplesearch, Findemails, Prophet, Kendo, Adorito, Preconnect tool, The Reach

ATS/CRM: Loxo, Hubspot, Tobu

Scraping: Zapinfo, Data Scraper, Instant Data Scraper

Writing Tools: Textio, Mosaic Track, JobLint, Readability, Spam, Humatic

Helper Tools: IP Whois, SideeX, Free VPN, WhenX, Clearbit, Pipl(Chrome Ext), Sales Search, Social Geek, Scroll it! tidy bookmarks, Custom Chrome Ext Mgr, Find My Bookmarks, Textly.AI, 360internetprotection, Free Email Hunter, Intelligence Search, Search Term Finder

Special:

https://start.me/p/GE7Ebm/ssar

https://start.me/p/aLAeEp/ssar-2

https://start.me/p/EL84Km/cse-utopia

https://start.me/p/NxRQbG/search-eng-utopia

Any tool, or site mentioned in this book can be found on one of the Start.me pages Mentioned in this book

Chapter 30

OSINT/SOCMINT Training and Certification

Simple put where you can go to get training and certifications for OSINT and SOCMINT. Keep in mind OSINT is used mainly in investigations so most training programs are designed for investigators.

I provide OSINT and SOCMINT training but mine is specific to Staffing, Recruiting and Sourcing. http://thesearchauthority.weebly.com/consulting-services.html

IntelTechniques provides OSINT training and certification

https://inteltechniques.com/training/ ** **I recommend this training, the best there is**

Netbootcamp also provides OSINT training

https://netbootcamp.org/trainingprogram/

UDEMY has several OSINT training programs

https://www.udemy.com

SANS provides OSINT Training live or online.

https://www.sans.org/course/open-source-intelligence-gathering

Cybrary has alot of free training on OSINT and more.

https://www.cybrary.it/

Tomoko Discovery has a number of OSINT, SOCMINT and other intelligence orientated training

https://tomokodiscovery.com/

Now there are others but these seem like the best and most cost efficient.

Chapter 31

What do I use?

In this book I have outlined alot of things. Any tool, category or site that has a ** next to it are things I use and prefer. All of the tools that I have given their own chapter to, I use and prefer. However, I want to take a minute to talk about the tools I use to mitigate the risk on the web.

So, for me if I am doing serious deep work, I start with a Sandbox environment. For me I use Shade, and within Shade I use Virtual box and then either work within OSIRT or Buscador and then of course utilize a VPN. All that said 99% of the time I work within Buscador, as it has nearly everything I need and I can add tools, sites, extensions, etc, to it.

If for some reason I am not doing serious work, but still deeper than every day work I use the Tor browser along with a VPN, but still in a sandboxed environment.

If I am doing everyday work, I will simply use a VPN.

Now keep in mind most of your internet providers have a level of security to the modems and routers you are using. Also be sure all your security software is up to date. Meaning firewall, antivirus, anti-phishing, malware etc are all up to date. If you do all this you will have done as much as you can to be as safe as you can.

Also, as it relates to extensions. If they are from the Chrome store they have gone through the Google security and safety protocols and have been approved for use. If they are from sites, Github or were ever they have not, so be very careful if you use them. Ensure you have ample browser security. For me that means the following: 360 Internet Security, Windows Defender Browser Security, and Blockwebsite Notifications. Added to the Chrome built in security, if you are up to date with latest version of Chrome and you should be fine

The crux of all this is "be careful."

Chapter 32

Gifts

So, this is the gifts part. I created 3 Start.me pages, 1 is "SA OSINT" this is where I have brought together my most liked OSINT stuff. The 2 is "Add-ons, Tools, & Ext Utopia" -a massive list of tools, add-ons, and extension to include OSINT tools, the 3rd is "OSINT UTOPIA" -this is an enormous listing of OSINT tools, they are not categorized, but nearly every OSINT tool you can think of is there. Now there is some redundancy between them, but there is alot specific to each page. They can't be found by searching, you can only get them with the links below, and you can only get the links by buying this book.

https://start.me/p/5vN2a0/sa-osint

https://start.me/p/jjLykn/addons-tools-ext-utopia

https://start.me/p/7kzDqv/osint-utopia-category

Keep in mind the OSINT Utopia is vast, so it can take time to load, and you may need to reload a time or two.

Final Thoughts

Once again keep in mind this is not a book to go in-depth on OSINT. This book is designed for a high level, cursory understanding of OSINT. With some tools and methods sprinkled in. However, as you saw in this book, alot of what we do in staffing with regards to the sourcing lifecycle involves alot of OSINT. If after reading this book, you go back to my first book "Recruiting Da Costa Style," you will see where some of the things you learned in this book fit. An example would be using Spiderfoot to find more information on someone when all you have is an email, that fits in enhancement in the sourcing lifecycle.

The tools that are OSINT are as many as the grains of sand on a beach so I chose not to go into all of them. Just a few, however, the sites in the gifts chapter give you access to alot of them. Now you know where they fit within OSINT, where to go, where not to go, and where all these fits in the sourcing lifecycle. Above all I leave you with one thing if you think the "Deep Web" is safe your wrong, truth be told no part of the web is safe but the lower you go, the less secure and safe it is. This book does tell you how to make it as safe as possible, though. You combine the knowledge of being as safe as possible with the tools you learned here and the sourcing lifecycle and you are set.

"May the Source be with you."

Made in United States
North Haven, CT
12 June 2023

37614095R10133